Betty Lou McBride

Ghosts
of the
Molly
Maguires?

A Decade of Strange &
Unusual Happenings
in The Old Jail
Jim Thorpe, PA

by

Betty Lou McBride

Kathleen McBride Sisack

For information or orders contact:

The Old Jail Museum
c/o Betty Lou McBride
802 Center Street
Jim Thorpe, PA 18229
570-325-3309
tomblm@verizon.net

Published by:
Maverickpublishing & Distribution
P.O. Box 578, Jim Thorpe, PA 18229

Printed by:
Christmas City Printing Co.
Bethlehem, PA 18018

ISBN 0-9715817-1-1

~ Acknowledgments ~

Thanks to the many people who have given us their personal or written testimony regarding the unexplained "happenings" in The Old Jail Museum & Heritage Center, Inc. This book would not have been possible without their stories.

Thanks also to the many people who have shared their photographs showing orbs, shadows and markings that they felt were important to the strange occurrences in the Old Jail Museum. A list of photographic contributors to this book appears on page 121.

Special thanks to my daughter, Kathleen McBride Sisack, who spent many hours putting this book into readable form.

And many thanks to my dear husband, Tom, whose idea it was to buy the jail and make it possible for all these great happenings to come to light.

~ Betty Lou McBride
  May 1, 2006

~ Dedication ~

The book is dedicated to whomever or whatever it is that people experience, feel, sense, hear or see in The Old Jail Museum. If they truly are spirits, may they find peace and an end to their roaming.

~ Contents ~

Chapter 1

Visitors of the Old Jail

Seen & Unseen

Face flushed and breathing heavily, the 35-year-old woman gingerly approached us to ask a question. She hesitated, looking perplexed, and started, "This is going to sound odd . . ." Little did we know that the question to follow would be one we would hear repeatedly over the next eleven years. In these pages you will hear first-hand accounts of the many unusual activities experienced by visitors to the Old Jail Museum—the many visitors who have asked us versions of that question we first heard over a decade ago: "Do other people feel strange things here, too?"

A woman's voice calling for help . . .
On an empty staircase.

Walking into a wall . . .
A wall that wasn't there.

People in cells . . .
Empty cells.

The sensation of people nearby . . .
People who could be felt but not seen.

Shortness of breath & difficulty in breathing . . .
For no apparent reason.

Hands on shoulders . . .
When no one was around.

Men playing cards . . .
Men who were not there.

Shadows in cells . . .
Where there was no light to cast a shadow.

A cell door closing itself . . .
When it is repeatedly left open.

A wisp of the scent of flowers . . .
In a cold, empty cell.

Strange and unusual experiences in the Old Jail Museum have been reported by numerous men, women, teenagers, and children coming from near and far, from all 50 states and from many foreign countries. Our visitors' experiences have run the gamut, from physical sensations of sight, sound, hearing and touch, to emotional feelings including fear, anger, confusion, foreboding and, even, calmness and peace.

Are there spirits in the Old Jail Museum? If yes, who are they (or who were they)? Why are they still here? Are they the ghosts of the Molly Maguires who were hanged in this jail so many years ago? Does the jail's connection with this 19th century Irish laborers' organization have anything to do with some visitors' unexplained encounters? Why do only some of the jail's visitors experience strange things? Are these feelings or experiences the result of paranormal activity or psychic phenomenon? Are they the result of active imaginations? I honestly don't know. The majority of the incidents related here have been personally recorded

Jail Curators: *Betty Lou and Thomas McBride have welcomed over 165,000 visitors since opening the Old Jail in 1995.*

by our staff, and a few have been recalled from the days when we did not keep written records of this type of unusual activity.

Once we realized how many visitors were approaching us with questions regarding their curious experiences, we started keeping track of the stories. We would jot down the tale, along with a description of the guest, date the paper and file it in a folder in a drawer (or in my husband Tom's case, in the pockets of whatever he was wearing that day). When this folder started to overflow with many scraps of paper, as well as lengthy letters received from visitors describing their experiences, we decided to compile the many tales and arrange them by date.

In addition to Tom and me, many guides have heard tales of unexplained happenings from visitors during the last 11 years—Amanda, Dolly, Ed, two guides named Bridget, Alicia, Matt, Ian, Christina,

July 1995
Two 12-year-old girls were excitedly whispering to each other while on a tour. One of the girls then told her guide, "There's a hand on my shoulder and I have terrible, terrible chills." As the tour approached the dungeon, her red-haired friend refused to go inside. Soon after, the guide again heard the girls whispering. "They're here," one girl said to the other, both girls now physically trembling.

Dan, Kate and Katie, two Taras, Alisa, Jeanine, Chad, Rodney, Chelsey, Ann, Lauren and many more. Some of these guides have also shared their own personal adventures at the jail.

For the first several years that we operated the jail as a museum, we concentrated solely on the historical aspects of the jail, most notably the jail's connection to the Molly Maguires. We did not want to promote the jail as a "haunted house," and we did not want to dilute the saga of the Molly Maguires. We instructed our guides not to tell their tours any stories about ghosts, and we even turned down a request by *Good Morning America* to be profiled as part of one of their Halloween episodes on haunted destinations.

But the perplexing stories kept coming. Two years ago, in response to numerous requests, we started giving special "Ghost Tours" around Halloween. These ghost tours, where visitors hear many of the stories that appear in the following pages, are in addition to our regular tours.

Our regular daily tours still focus on the historical aspects of the jail, and we do not mention the rooms in which other visitors have had unusual experiences. We always let our visitors tell us where they feel or see something unusual. In fact, over the years a change in the pattern of reported experiences or feelings has occurred. In the first few years reports of strange or uncomfortable sensations were nu-

---

August 7, 2005
Guide Tara was in the dungeon waiting for her tour to come down the stairs from the cell block when suddenly she heard the shuffle of feet on the dirty floor and felt someone near her. "It sounded like someone was dragging his feet and it made a loud noise right beside me." Turning to see who was there, she found she was alone, as her group had not yet descended the stairs.

---

merous—about two or three reportings per week. Then for several years the reportings were less frequent. Recently, for some reason, we are again hearing from visitors several times a week about their unusual and unexplained sensations.

Neither my husband nor I has had major experiences of anything strange in the building in the years that we've owned the jail. On one or two occasions we have each had what might be called a "feeling" of someone else in the room, but not much else. We have watched with intrigue as the reports of the unusual happenings grow in frequency, and we have wondered why some people experience these feelings and others do not. Our three daughters, Peggy, Kathleen and Michelle, visit the Old Jail on a regular basis and have not had any unusual or uncomfortable experiences. Our daughter, Kathleen, even spent time on a Halloween evening photographing all areas of the jail. (She had heard that this should be an active time for spirits). She neither saw nor felt anything unusual, and her pictures yielded no surprises—and no orbs. We have been told over the years that most of the presences in the jail are happy that we bought the building and they want to protect us.

Motion detector cameras, digital photography and infrared videography (to capture anomalous images), infrared thermometers and thermal registers (to check for hot and cold spots), audio recording devices (to record EVPs, electronic voice phenomena), and elec-

July 1995
With the fall theater season and a play about the Molly Maguires approaching, a group of young actors came to see where the Molly Maguires had been hanged so the actors could portray these men with a greater level of understanding. Several of the young people were not particularly interested in the saga of the Molly Maguires but came simply for a day of sight-seeing. One of the non-interested actors wanted to take photos of some of the others in front of Cell 17 but was frustrated when his camera wouldn't work. He tried and tried, but to no avail; he could not get the camera to function. We suggested he move the subjects to the other side of the cell block and try again. This time his camera worked perfectly .

Just then an actress who was knowledgeable about Molly Maguires and sympathetic to their plight decided to take pictures in front of Cell 17. As she posed her friends in front of the cell everyone told her to move because her camera would not work But to everyone's surprise, she had no trouble with her camera while taking several pictures.

tromagnetic field detectors (to observe the electrostatic field) have all been used by students of parapsychology and paranormal activities in attempts to capture the cause of the unexplained and mysterious activity in the Old Jail. All of these terms (and instruments) were foreign to us just a few years ago, and we don't pretend to understand any of it. Some investigators succeeded on a limited basis by finding lights and digital orbs, but most people searching for ghosts in the Old Jail have not found them. Interestingly, it is most often the unaware or non-searching visitor who experiences an unusual sensation or phenomenon.

Many visitors have taken pictures in the Old Jail that have shown orbs

The Massive Front Door "Welcomes" Visitors to the Old Jail:
Weighing approximately 1,000 lbs., the door is composed of three layers of oak and one layer of sheet iron. The original front door remains intact; all fixtures and locks are original.

floating in many different rooms in the building. These round balls of white are thought by some paranormal investigators to be visible signs of spirits, while others feel that orbs are nothing more than dust particles. Over the past decade we have seen dozens of unusual photos: people have returned to the jail with pictures; they have mailed or e-mailed them to us; visitors have even stopped after tours to show us pictures still in their cameras. And many contain these distinct orbs. Oddly, none of the pictures taken by our family over the years has ever contained an orb.

Through the years, the stone walls of the Old Jail have witnessed much sadness and distress. An untold number of men and women have been confined behind these cold, iron bars in the 135 years since the jail was built. And a number of people too large to count have visited, laughed and more importantly, cried with these men and women over these many years. For the past 11 years now, a new set of

Broadway: Downtown Jim Thorpe is home to many fine shops, galleries and restaurants. The Old Jail is located further up Broadway.

visitors have been making their way through the oak and iron doors of the Old Jail. The overall tone of the jail has changed from one of negativity and solitude to one of history and tourism. Even though the role of the jail has changed from an active prison to an historical museum, visitors will always be reminded of the men and woman who lived and died inside these walls. There are many stories from inside these walls, and it seems that visitors from the past are eager to relate some of these stories to visitors of today.

This casual compilation of the experiences of our visitors is presented now for your enjoyment, amazement and disbelief. It is offered simply as a book of entertaining stories. We do not make any claims as to the reality of the narratives. We have not, however, fabricated or enhanced any of the stories, nor have we digitally altered the strange images that appear in the photos on the following pages. Read on and see what you think. *What is that cold chill? Whose hands are those on your shoulders? Who is making that scratching noise? What is that orb in the photograph? Are there spirits in the Old Jail Museum? Are these the spirits of the Molly Maguires?*

~ Chapter 2 ~

Broadway Bastille
A History of the Old Jail

R esembling a fortress standing guard over the town of Jim Thorpe, Pennsylvania (formerly known as Mauch Chunk), the historic Old Jail Museum is a two-story structure with thick, massive walls and a formidable watch tower. Completed in 1871, the jail is constructed of hand-cut stone and is set into the side of the rocky mountain so that it once looked to be part of the mountain itself.

An outstanding example of 19th century prison architecture, the 72 room jail was designed by Edward Haviland, son of John Haviland, architect of the Eastern State Penitentiary in Philadelphia. The ornamental wrought iron railing around the front of the building is formed in the pattern of a knotted rope so even the fence serves as a symbol of containment.

The entire front portion of the building was the warden's living quarters complete with a living room, dining room, three bedrooms, sitting room, bathroom and kitchen. From 1871 to 1970 each warden and his family lived inside the jail. The prison component of the building is comprised of 25 cells in the main cell block (12 on the first floor, and 13 on the second floor), 16 dank dungeon cells (used as solitary confinement of prisoners until 1980), and three separate women's cells on the second floor.

Through the years the jail has been the site of many deaths, both through capital punishment and as a result of suicide. In the late 1800s, the common mode of capital punishment was by hanging and the jail held a central role in the hanging of many men. The gallows were erected in the back of the main cell block, which allowed for many onlookers to gather around the balcony and on the staircase to witness the executions.

~ The Handprint on the Wall ~

During the late 1800s many Irish families came to this area to escape the horrors of life in Ireland leaving behind hardship, evictions, potato famine and starvation. They came hoping to find a better life on the golden shores of America. Eventually many of these new immigrants found work in the coal mines, only to discover that mining was extremely dangerous because of the numerous cave-ins, fires and explosions. It did not take the men long to realize the coal companies were more interested in making money than they were in protecting the lives of the miners. To add to their problems they were not paid a

Instrument of Death: *A recreation of the gallows, large enough to hang four people simultaneously, stands in the main cell block.*

decent day's wages for their long hours in the dark mines and the men soon found the coal mining companies were in control of their lives.

In order to better their lives the miners began forming a union that was strongly resented by the coal or railroad companies because higher wages and safer working conditions would lessen their profits. When the coal companies tried to eliminate the union activists, mayhem broke out. Any and all troubles in the coal fields and the murders of coal

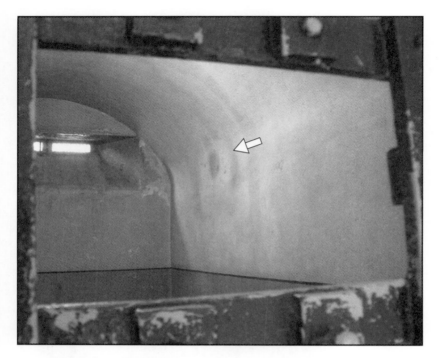

Image from the Past: *This mysterious "handprint on the wall" appeared more than 120 years ago and, despite repeated attempts to remove it, can still be seen today.*

bosses were blamed on a group called the Molly Maguires, said to be a secret society of miners who battled the exploitation of the mine owners.

On June 21, 1877, four coal miners, all accused of murder and alleged to be Molly Maguires, were hanged at one time on the gallows built at the rear of the main cell block of the jail. They were Alexander Campbell, Edward Kelly, Michael Doyle, and John Donohue. Within the next one and one-half years three more miners were hanged in the jail. On March 28, 1878, the hangman's noose tightened around the neck of Thomas P. Fisher and on January 14, 1879, James McDonnell and Charles Sharp were the final two men to have their lives end on this notorious "instrument of death."

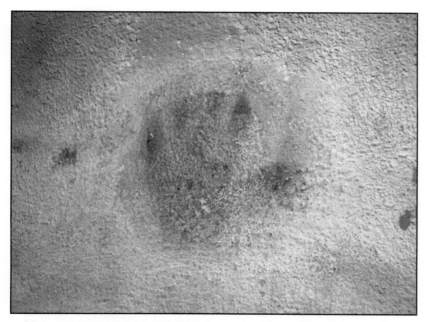

Mark of Innocence: *Close-up view of the handprint on the wall of Cell 17.*

Some people now believe the organization of the Molly Maguires never existed. It is accepted that many individual miners were working for betterment though the unions, but not by means of an official organization. It is now known that a private corporation, the Philadelphia and Reading Coal Company, played a key role in the Molly Maguire case: they initiated the investigation through a private detective agency, the Pinkerton Detective Agency; they used a private police force, the Coal and Iron Police, to capture the accused men; they dismissed the state's prosecutors; and they hired private coal company attorneys to prosecute the miners. Today's historians feel the Molly Maguires were unjustly accused and their trials were a surrender of state sovereignty because the State of Pennsylvania provided only the courtroom in which the men were tried and the gallows upon which the men met their final fate.

Today, many believe these condemned men were falsely accused of murder and unjustly hanged. On December 5, 2005, Pennsylvania

7/24/2000
Letter regarding the handprint on the wall:

"I recently attended the family reunion in Mauch Chunk. My nephew expressed to me your interest in the documentation about the handprint in the jail. My father, Albertus Herman, a mason contractor, was the person who chiseled out the mark of the hand in the cell at least four times I know of. He was employed by Neast &Co. to do the work. I cannot give exact dates as I was young at the time. It would have been during the late 20s or 30s.

I remember begging to go along as I wanted to see it. He re-cemented it and each time when the cement was dry the hand mark reappeared ... Hope this will help you for your documentation. It is definitely true. I can so vividly remember him coming away from a phone call saying, 'I have to go to the jail and chisel out the hand again'. Why can't people accept it as fact."

Respectfully,
Mrs. EHK, Florida

House of Representatives passed House Resolution No. 527, "Recognizing the lack of due process in the 1876-1878 trials of several alleged members of the Molly Maguires and memorializing the Governor to issue an order acknowledging the same."

Most of the hanged coal miners declared their innocence, but two men made the declaration in a very specific manner. Alexander Campbell, a 40-year-old coal miner and the owner of the Columbia House Hotel in Storm Hill, Landsford, PA, proclaimed his innocence before he was hanged in 1877. And 40-year-old Thomas P. Fisher, also a coal miner and the owner of the Rising Sun Hotel in Summit Hill, PA, stated before his hanging in 1879: "A century from now this Mauch Chunk prison will be an historical landmark. I am innocent. When the day of my execution comes I will let the public know that I am an innocent man . . ."

To add to this tale of prejudice and servitude local folklore brings us more mystery. It is said that before his hanging one of the condemned men placed his hand on the dirty floor of his cell and then put it firmly on the cell wall. He proclaimed his handprint would stay on the wall as an eternal sign of his innocence and his unjust execution. Today, this mysterious handprint remains on the wall of Cell 17 of the Old Jail for everyone to see, and that particular cell continues to evoke numerous unexplained feelings and happenings.

No one knows for sure who placed this testimony to injustice on the wall of Cell 17, but most people and authors believe it to be one of the two men originally hailing from County Donegal: Alexander Campbell or Thomas Fisher. And no one knows why Cell 17 affects so many people today.

The wall with the handprint has been washed and painted with fresh paint numerous times. The handprint has also been dug out and the wall replastered. In 1975 the National Inquirer commissioned a scientific investigation of this strange phenomenon; Dr. Jeffrey T. Cline, a geologist of Wilkes University in Wilkes-Barre, PA, examined the handprint. Samples of the handprint and wall were analyzed in a gas chromatograph, a device used to determine the chemical composition of organic materials. The analysis showed no traces of grease what-soever. Only the paint on the wall showed up in the tests. Dr. Cline stated, "If the print is not a grease mark, then there is no logical explanation for its persistence on the wall."

~ New Routine for the Jail ~

From 1871 until January 1995 the jail served as the Carbon County Prison. In January 1995 we, Tom and Betty Lou McBride of Jim Thorpe, PA, purchased the former Carbon County Prison from the Commissioners of Carbon County. We planned to preserve the heritage of the jail, to continue the memory of the Molly Maguires, and to protect the famous "handprint of innocence" on the wall.

But we had absolutely no idea what we were going to do with this historic building while preserving it. After all, who would be interested in seeing an old jail? We decided to open the jail for tours and see what would happen. We also wanted to designate an area to be used as a depository for historical documents and memorabilia about the Molly Maguires. The county moved the prisoners to the new prison four miles away in January 1995 and within two weeks they had removed all the prison materials and equipment. The building was ours!

Restoration work progressed at a feverish pace. Tom had previously restored several other historic buildings in the Old Mauch Chunk Historic District of Jim Thorpe, we had opened a general gift and Irish import shop called The Treasure Shop in downtown Jim Thorpe, and we now wanted to bring this magnificent stone edifice back to life.

While we were completing the restoration of the jail, we researched the building and its connection to the men known as the Molly Magu-

Hands-On: *Tom and Betty Lou McBride restored the warden's rooms of the Old Jail before opening the building for public tours.*

ires. This was all new and exciting to us both and we became deeply involved with the story of the Irish immigrant miners who began the first organized unions in the anthracite coal regions. Tours were planned, scripts written, signs made, and publicity started. The Old Jail Museum opened for its first visitors in May 1995, just four months after the last prisoners left. Visitors coming into the building had no idea of what they would see or what to expect when coming through the gigantic, 1,000 lb. front door.

Come with us now as we take you through the Old Jail by way of strange experiences related by visitors. Some of these reports are very unusual and fearful while others are quite simple. But they are all true! Many reports seem to repeat themselves. As I was editing the stories, I often thought, "Oh, I've recorded that story already," only to find the date of the event I was typing was about five years after the

Dedication: *Original cut stone dedication sign over front door of the Old Jail. Note misspelling of architect Edward Haviland's name.*

one I remembered. The manifestation was the same, just different people and different dates.

These episodes have followed a definite pattern as to location and type of person having the experience. And the strange or unusual feelings and emotions are felt in similar locations in the building. The visitors whose stories are narrated here did not know each other, and they did not know that other people had also experienced unusual and sometimes frightening events in this building. They came to us with that famous question, *"Am I the only one who feels strange things in here?"*

~ Outside the Jail ~

We don't hear much about visitors experiencing any strange activity outside the jail. And we have only one recent report of unusual activity in the exercise yard adjacent to the jail. Moreover, on the few occasions when inside lights and images have been glimpsed from the outside, it has always been neighbors or guides who have noticed and reported them.

Fortress on the Hill: *Built in 1871, the hand-cut stone jail stands guard over the town of Jim Thorpe, PA.*

July 22, 2002

Two young guides at the Old Jail were walking down the street (West Broadway) one night after dark. As they passed the jail they noticed a light on in a second story window. "We knew no one was there because it was too late. When we looked longer, we both were surprised to see a man sitting in the window in something red. When we told Mr. and Mrs. McBride what we saw, they told us that no one was in the building at that hour but that several other neighbors reported that they, too, had seen the man sitting upstairs in the window."

~ The Warden's Living Area ~

The rooms that comprised the warden's apartment are located across the front of the building on both the first and second floors. On the

Before: *Fireplace in warden's living room before restoration.*
This fireplace opening was found behind paneling during renovation.

first floor, just inside the front door are the living room, dining room and kitchen. The kitchen is adjacent to the cell block because meals for both the warden's family and the prisoners were prepared in it. In 1970 when the warden no long resided in the jail these rooms were changed from personal living areas to jail offices or prisoner-use rooms. The warden's living room became the guards' office, the dining room became a storage room, and the bedrooms became a separate section to house work release prisoners. The living room and dining room are now restored to reflect the time around 1900.

The children of the last warden tell delightful tales of playing in the hallways and riding their tricycles around and around through the first floor living area. Other family members tell of the teenage parties that they enjoyed in these rooms. This was a typical family home with family dinners and children's toys, Christmas trees and birthday parties. The daughter of one warden had her wedding pictures taken on the front steps of the prison, while another daughter said that when

After: Restored living room fireplace during the grand opening celebration.

she was a child she thought she was Cinderella because she lived in a grand house with a guard at her front door. There have been relatively few reports of unusual happenings in these rooms in comparison to the rooms in which prisoners were incarcerated.

So, we will begin our tales here and wend our way through the many seemingly "empty" rooms of the Old Jail. The following narratives are presented as they were told or written to us. We have tried to remain as objective and impartial as possible in recording these events, and any of our own speculations are printed in italics.

1995
One of the Old Jail's first visitors was a woman who spent a long time in the warden's living room. She was curious because she could feel a small white dog roaming around under her feet.

May 1995
We were hurrying to get ready for our first visitors and I was cleaning the Visitors' Room. Suddenly I was surprised to feel someone behind me. I spun around only to find no one there. My heart was beating fast and furious because I knew my husband was the only other person in the building and he was in another room. What had I felt? Was it just my imagination or was some- one or something actually watching me?

May 1995
As a group of visitors passed through a hall, adjacent to the main cell block, they were hit by a horrible, disgusting smell. The strangest aspect of this smell was that it could not be detected in the first five feet of this hall nor was it in the last five feet. It was a great concern to us because we had just opened the museum and could not figure out what was causing this pungent odor. We unsuccessfully tried various fragrance sprays and deodorizers. After about a week the odor dissi- pated with no source ever detected; it never returned in this location. Later, the same smell did appear in another hallway for a two week period and then it disappeared forever (we hope).

May 2000
The Carbon County Commissioners were in the process of selecting an organization to replace the Carbon County Tourist Promotion Agency to handle the tourism aspects for Carbon County and Jim Thorpe. Within the business community there was much disagree- ment as to whether the Carbon County Tourist Promotion Agency should be retained or whether it should be replaced with the Pocono Mountains Vacation Bureau. A meeting regarding this changeover was held at the Old Jail. During the evening, discussion was heated and emotions flared.

Both Tom and I were not in favor of the takeover at that time. At one point in the intense discussion Tom left the room. When he didn't return I became alarmed and went to check on him. He was standing in the hallway just outside the door and said he was "unable to return

Stairway from the Warden's Quarters: *From 1871 to 1970 each warden lived with his family in the jail. The entire front portion of the building was the warden's living quarters complete with living room, dining room, three bedrooms, sitting room, bathroom and kitchen.*

to the room." He said he wanted to come back in, but "simply could not return." He had no idea why he felt this way.

Normally I am quite excitable and yet during this heated evening I remained strangely calm. My emotions didn't rise, my voice was quiet and I remember just sitting and listening. Our daughter, Peggy, was taking minutes of the meeting and noted later that she couldn't understand why I was so quiet and not involved in the discussion since I had very strong feelings on the subject. As I sat there I kept thinking, "Why am I so calm? This is so unusual for me."

Three months later Tom was hospitalized for emergency heart surgery. The doctors said that any stressful event during the preceding few months could have triggered a heart attack. Thinking back to that tense night at the jail, one of our daughters "joked" that possibly the unseen forces in the building had inhibited me from my usual emotional arguments (it upsets Tom to see me so agitated) and the same forces had prevented Tom from returning to the room with the upsetting debate.

May 21, 2005

Kelli had come for a tour and was waiting in the warden's living room when she was startled by the smell of very strong cigarette or cigar smoke. In looking around, she saw no one smoking and she noticed that all the windows were tightly closed. As she snapped pictures in the living room, she found she was having trouble breathing. Later, when she looked at her digital pictures, she saw two separate orbs in the pictures taken in the living room.

~ Chapter 3 ~

Corridor
of Mysteries

The Main Cell Block

There have been relatively few changes in the main cell block since it first opened for prisoners in 1871. The 25 cells run along both sides of a long main corridor. Although measuring only 8 ft. x 13 ft. each cell can accommodate up to four prisoners within its narrow confines. The cells are bare: a toilet, sink, two to four bunks and a small, highly placed window measuring 6" x 32" are the only amenities. Originally each cell was secured by two doors: the inside door made of 2" wide iron bands in a lattice work pattern and locked with a bar and padlock; and the thick oak outer door that locked with this same padlock. The oak doors have no opening so a prisoner was completely isolated inside the cell when this door was closed.

Walls 24" thick, black slate floors and a very high skylight ceiling give the entire cell block an intimidating, foreboding look. Today, this cell block remains much as it was in the late 1800s when the accused Molly Maguires were confined and hanged within its walls. Moreover, the cell block also reflects the austere jail life of 20th century prisoners who were incarcerated in these barren cells as recently as 1995 when a new prison was erected.

In 1998, a reproduction of the original gallows was built at the far end of the cell block in almost the exact spot where the original gallows had once stood. The construction design was adapted from original 1871 newspapers detailing the hanging of four of the Molly Maguires.

~ Guards Tales from the Cell Block ~

Before we bought the jail we heard two intriguing stories from former guards. We didn't realize then that this would be just a sample of what was to come. We often wonder how many other stories have been told, or not told, by the former guards or in-mates about odd experiences within the jail's four stone walls.

Around 1970
In order to bring the jail up to fire code standards, concrete was poured over the wood floor in each cell except for the floor in Cell 17 which is the cell with the mysterious handprint on the wall. Interestingly, the floor of this cell was not changed and the original wood floor remained. Because of the wood floor the cell was not up to code and prisoners were not to be placed in this cell. Even so, one day a very difficult prisoner was brought into the prison and placed in Cell 17. We were told that the man screamed because he saw two people walking through the closed and bolted iron door of his cell. After about three hours, the man was moved to another cell.

Who did the prisoner see walking through that door? Was it the man who placed his handprint on the wall before his hanging? Was it Alexander Campbell? Or Thomas P. Fisher? Or another Molly Maguire?

Sometime before 1995:
One night two guards were making their regular rounds after visiting hours. One guard noticed two men on the second floor of the cell block sitting and playing cards. He asked another guard, "Why are there still two visitors here?" The other guard replied, "What are you

FiRst FlooR Cell Block

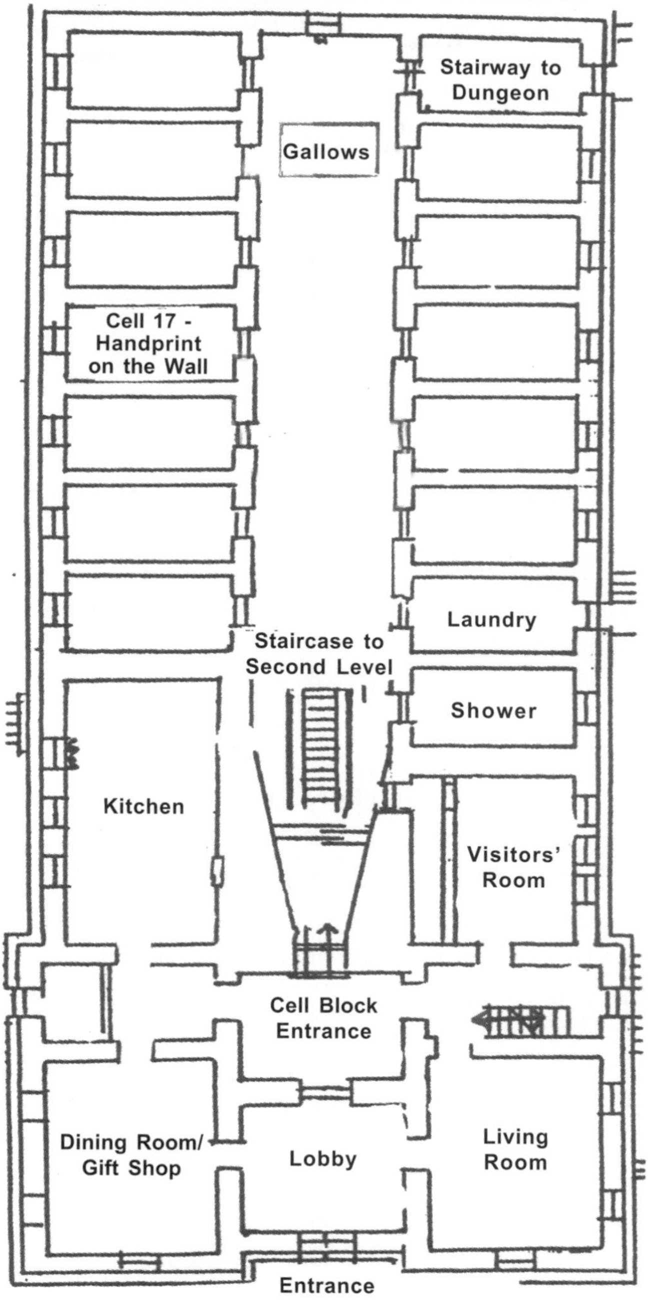

Stairway to
Dungeon

Gallows

Cell 17 -
Handprint
on the Wall

Laundry

Staircase to
Second Level

Shower

Kitchen

Visitors'
Room

Cell Block
Entrance

Dining Room/
Gift Shop

Lobby

Living
Room

Entrance

talking about? There are no visitors still in the building. Everyone is gone." "Well, come and tell me who these two men are," demanded the first guard. But, when they returned to the spot where the first guard had seen the two card players, no one was there.

Date unknown
The prisoners in Cell 24 often played cards in the evening and afterwards would stack the cards and put them on a stand. In the morning the prisoners would find the cards strewn around the floor, even though they had not touched them and their cell door had been securely locked all night.

~ Tales From the Lower Cell Block ~

For 124 years this stone building had served as a prison, complete with its rotating prisoners, employees and visitors. Now, for the first time, its doors were being opened to the general public, and the dynamics within these walls would be forever changed. We would soon discover that some of our unsuspecting visitors would be forever changed as well.

July 1995
An actress in plays about the Molly Maguires, Jill wanted to see the place where the Molly Maguires had been hanged. She and a friend were just about finished with the tour when she stopped suddenly. " I didn't realize I had stopped walking until Scott told me to keep walking. I had an overwhelming sense of sadness from within myself and I was in tears. It was so sad."

July 20, 1995
A mother, her daughter and the mother's sister came for a tour, but the mother decided she could not enter the jail. After the tour the daughter and her aunt both said separately that they had felt severe depression in several areas of the cell block.

April 1995

Washing the years of accumulated grime and smoke from the walls and ceiling of the guards' office, originally the warden's living room, was an extremely tiring job. Occasionally I would take a break from cleaning and go into the cell block and stand on the second floor at the top of the cast iron staircase. Gazing into the cell block, my thoughts would turn to the men who had died there and I would remember they were real men, not storybook figures or TV characters. These were real men, flesh and blood men with hopes, dreams, and fears!

One day while standing on the second floor balcony I saw a tiny, white light flash from left to right across the far end of the cell block. It reminded me of what our daughters used to call Tinkerbell's magic light when my husband would catch the sunlight on his knife during breakfast and make the tiny beam of light dance around the room. "Tinkerbell!" "Tinkerbell!", our young daughters would squeal with delight. This was the same kind of tiny light that I saw that day. I thought it must be a reflection from a truck passing in the street because the front door of the jail was open.

Later on, I realized that no light could have reflected off a passing vehicle, up a flight of stairs, through the narrow jail doorway, through two rooms, through two more sets of doors, past the iron staircase, and end up at the back end of the cell block just when I was standing there. But . . . if it was not a reflection, what did I see? No one was in the building but me and there was nothing in the cell block to create a moving light.

— Betty Lou McBride

September 29, 1995
Mary of Wynnewood, PA, toured the Old Jail with her family and later wrote us a letter describing her experiences on Dolly's tour.

"Finally we were there (the cell block). The guide led my brother, my daughter and her friend into the main room. I followed behind, pausing to read some items at the entrance. Then as I went to enter the room, I found that I had trouble walking. I was on the right side of the staircase. So I just walked around to the left side. Again I could not pass. It was not any thought in my mind or even a feeling that prevented me from going further. It was my body itself. I forced myself to move with great difficulty and once away from the stairs the difficulty lessened. I felt like crying and wanted to leave. I did not tell any of the others of this strange experience.

As I walked slowly into the cell block, I again walked into a wall. I walked right into it — but there was no wall there. I was not hurt, but surprised to see there was no wall yet I could not move forward.

Being Irish I am accustomed to pushing ahead no matter what. I forced myself to move, with great difficulty. Once I was a sufficient distance from the stairs the difficulty lessened but the emotions remained. I felt like crying and wanted to leave. It felt wrong being there.

My daughter was trying to tell me something as the guide was talking and I was annoyed because I wanted to hear what the guide was saying. They went ahead to the place where the hanging took place. I tried to go, but I hit a wall. Walked right into it. I wasn't hurt or anything and I felt no emotion, just an inability to proceed. The only thing is, there was no wall— only space. I made myself walk.

Do you know what it is to be unable to move? To will your body forward and to have your legs behave like a little puppy refusing to budge? I have never in my life been unable to move. At the end of the cell block I could move freely. It was almost a relief to go down the stairs to the dark dungeon. I felt relief to get away from that upstairs horror.

I started ahead of my brother going up the cell block stairs to the second floor but again I did not want to move. I told my brother to just go ahead of me and it made it easier. Once up the stairs I could move freely. Until I hit another wall full force! I had to hold onto the wooden railing that went around the cell block and I forced myself to walk. At one point my daughter went by me with no trouble and that was the only time I was afraid. I just could not let go of that railing! I looked ridiculous. My knees were buckling as I walked. Luckily it stopped by the time I got to the end but then it started again once I got to the first cell from the back. The weird walk stopped when I reached the spot where it had started.

My daughter and her friend are very skeptical of everything. I knew they thought I was the weirdest!."

Sincerely, Mary

August 20, 1995
This was a very active day for the spirits. A total of seven people ranging in age from 14 to 65 experienced strange and perplexing feelings all on this one day. This is just one of the accounts:

As their tour progressed, a mother from Palmerton, PA, felt chills and had to leave the building. Although experiencing "great sadness," her daughter continued on the tour.

September 1995
"I can see people in there," insisted a man from Hazleton, PA, "When I look in that cell I see two people inside." We assured him that Cell 17's door is always locked and no one is allowed inside. Later, when he viewed the photographs he had taken of the cell block for a promotional tape, he saw three ghost-like figures in the photos.

September 1995
"It's like having a roller coaster in my stomach," said a young girl from Mahanoy City School in Mahanoy City, PA, about her feelings during her tour. None of her schoolmates had felt anything strange during this same tour.

September 1995
One day a Catholic priest and his sister who live near Bethlehem, PA, visited and we chatted with them for a while. We then walked with them into the cell block where they both stopped abruptly as they "hit a wall of air." With seemingly great difficulty, they continued to walk around the cell block, blessing themselves many times. A short time later the sister felt weak and needed to be helped to a chair. Both the priest and his sister felt what they described as "depression and sadness" throughout the building.

September 9, 1995
As two college students walked to the back of the cell block, they had "unearthly feelings" such as they had never felt before. They had no

Hanging Around: *Visitors read placards in the main cell block. At least four orbs can also be seen throughout the photo.*

idea what caused these feelings—feelings each student described as "freaky."

1998

Alicia stopped her tour just outside the door to the cell block to check that the previous tour group had moved on from the cell block. She pulled open the door to glance inside, and as she did, a young girl on her tour looked past her to the gallows at the far end and quietly asked, "Why are there four men hanging up there?" Startled, Alicia quickly turned to look at the gallows, but there was no one on the gallows.

May 2, 1998

"Help me, help me," a young girl heard a woman call to her in the cell block. The girl did not appear to be frightened, just surprised, as she

Ghostly Silhouette: *One of our visitors snapped this picture and later discovered a dark shape in the background (next to the American flag) that was not there when he took the picture.*

asked us about the woman. When we told her that there was no woman there, the young girl insisted that the woman had long blond hair and a very white face. She said the woman was not doing anything special; she was just speaking to her. This young girl would not believe us when we told her again that there was no woman.

July 1998

Kathleen and her husband, from California, stopped in the gift shop to bring us proof of their strange adventure. Kathleen, her husband and her mother had been on a tour a few weeks earlier and had taken photos throughout the jail. She told us they had taken a picture of her mother standing in front of the first picnic table in the main cell block. When the photograph was developed they received a great surprise. Everything was in the photograph—except the mother! There was a white space in the photograph where the mother should have been. It appeared as if she had been just cut out of the picture. They assured us that this was the way the photo had come back from the developer, and they had done nothing to alter or enhance the image. *(See the picture on the opposite page.)*

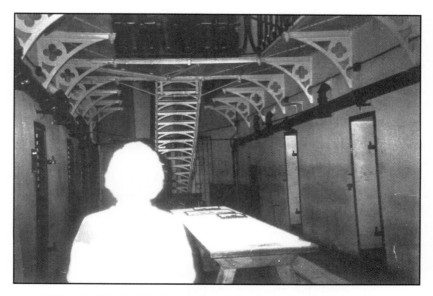

Where's Mom? *A California woman took a photo of her mother, but she received a surprise when the film was developed— the mother was not in the picture.*

August 1998

A man told Tom that we were wrong in saying the mysterious, 135-year-old handprint belonged to Alexander Campbell or to Thomas Fisher. This man said it was the handprint of Michael Doyle.

October 1998

The Old Jail was extremely busy with visitors who had come to Jim Thorpe to see the breathtaking fall foliage. In the midst of the regular tours of that day about 100 Brownie Scouts came to see the jail. Our regular visitors, plus the Brownies, meant that an extremely large number of people were in the building at one time creating a great deal of noise and confusion. Later that day, the mother of one of the Brownies called to ask if any guides had dressed in period costumes to playfully scare the children. We told her we had been so busy giving tours that none of the guides would have had time for play-acting, plus we would never want to scare children so young. She then told us her daughter's story:

When her daughter returned home from her troop's visit to the jail, she nonchalantly mentioned to her mother that she had seen a woman in a white dress with long blond hair standing at the bottom of the iron staircase in the cell block. "Help me, help me, " she heard the woman in the white dress call. The girl told her mother she had not been frightened, but that she was curious about the woman.

October 1998
The wail of bagpipes could be heard throughout the cell block as the piper stood near the gallows. His wife, who had accompanied him to the Old Jail, was seated nearby. Because we were pleased to have the piper playing, our staff joined in listening to the soulful music. As we listened we noticed that the piper's wife was in tears. We talked with her after the bagpipe selections were over, and she told us that while her husband was playing she had heard a woman crying—actually wailing—in the area of the cells. She explained that it was the despair of this unseen crying woman that had caused her to become so emotional.

October 1998
A young girl and her father had been looking in different cells. Her father told us that his daughter had come to him very annoyed, saying, "Tell that man with the red scarf on his head inside that cell to stop staring at me!" The father said he looked in the cell but saw no one.

A few days later, Heather, a guide, mentioned this incident to a former prison guard who happened to stop by the jail for a tour. This guard told her that he remembered that a prisoner who often wore a red bandana had committed suicide in the jail many years ago. He remembered the incident so well because when he entered the cell to retrieve the dead man's body the cell mate informed him, "I'm going to commit suicide, too." The guard remembered sarcastically replying, "Well, hurry up, so I can take both bodies out at the same time." (The second prisoner did not commit suicide.)

Locked Up: *The small handcuff door, above, was unlocked and opened to allow guards to place handcuffs on inmates before opening the adjacent door. The jail's front door, above right, has the original lock still in place. A typical cell door, right, has a heavy sliding lock.*

October 20, 1998

As a group composed of dancers and musicians progressed through the building, one of the musicians said he could no longer stay in the building and hurriedly left. Several other members of the tour felt strange emotions and feelings throughout the building. One of the dancers was seen in tears as she sat in the cell block looking at the gallows.

October 20, 1998

A husky man with long, light brown hair and wearing work clothes came into the Old Jail to inquire about another stone building in Jim Thorpe. He was a stone mason from Arizona, possibly of German or Polish descent, and had been employed to duplicate the Jim Thorpe stone building in Arizona. We discussed the building he was seeking and I asked him if he wanted to see the stone work of the Old Jail building. As we walked around looking at the stone, we passed the cell entrance where I pointed out the cell block and suggested he go inside. I had said nothing about the gallows nor the handprint. He slowly looked around and then walked up the left side of the cell block. As he got to the informational signs at Cell 17 he did not even glance at them. He stopped suddenly, remarking "I feel very strange." He turned to me and said it was like someone had hit him or shoved him in the chest.

When I suggested he, as a stone mason, might be interested in seeing the handprint on the wall of Cell 17, he shouted, "No way, man! I have to get out of this place!" He immediately hurried back to the gift shop where he told guides Charlotte, Catherine, and Jennifer what he had just experienced.

I asked him if he wanted to go out to the parking lot through the side door but he said," No, I'll go out the same door I came in." Catherine laughed saying that was an old Irish superstition. He firmly said, "I'm not Irish", and hurried to the front door. As I asked him to wait so I could get him a brochure he said, "No, way. I'll never come back here again. I'm ready to head back to Arizona!"

July 1999
All of a sudden a young girl on Ian's tour appeared very agitated. She had seen the profile of a person's shoulder and arm in the first cell on the left.

July 1999
Tom D. was standing in the area in front of the gallows when he felt a tightness in his throat and neck. He was not alarmed but did not know what caused the feeling. He also had the sensation that the original gallows may have been placed slightly more forward than the reconstructed gallows. *Tom D. had no way of knowing that the*

location of the original gallows was indeed slightly more toward the center of the cell block to allow more room for the rear stairs ascending the gallows. In recreating the gallows we chose to have them built without stairs for safety reasons.

August 1999

As Debora B. peered through the bars of the iron door into Cell 17 to see the handprint she could sense someone in the cell. She felt there was a man in the cell sitting on a chair, leaning against the back wall and watching

Surrounded by Orbs: *Jen from Bethlehem, PA, thought she was having her picture taken alone. The enlargements of the orbs appear on the following pages.*

the visitors as they looked at the handprint. This man, she explained, feels as if he is an actor earning his pay as he watches the visitors peer inside his cell. She said he does not mind that he is there, but she was not sure if he was the man who placed the handprint on the wall.

After talking with Debora, Tom suggested she walk around the cell block a bit more. He and three guides watched as she slowly walked

Surrounded by Orbs: *Enlarged detail from the picture on page 39.*

up six or eight steps of the staircase to the second floor of the cell block. Suddenly, she hesitated, then slowly walked up two more steps, only to hesitate again. She paused for a moment, then proceeded up the remainder of the stairs to the library.

Debora recounted that as she went up the stairs she had heard someone wailing and had the uneasy sensation that someone was watching her. She then heard a woman's voice screaming, "I'm too late, I'm too late." Debora described this woman as wearing heavy, dark clothes and having rough-red hands. She felt the woman had often come in through the front door of the jail and at one time had rushed into the cell block and up the stairs. She said the screaming woman almost fainted in anguish and she (Debora) had to come back downstairs to get out of that area.

Debora did not know that in 1879 a very distraught Mrs. Charles Sharpe had entered the jail just after her husband's hanging as a Molly Maguire and had rushed up these same stairs. That morning Governor Roudenbush had granted a five-day stay of execu-

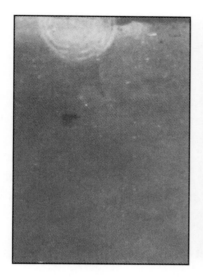

More Orbs: Close-ups of the orbs from the picture on page 39.

tion to Charles Sharpe and James McDonnell. When Mrs. Sharpe, accompanied by the telegraph operator who was delivering the stay of execution for Sharpe and McDonnell, knocked at the prison door the warden refused their entry saying, "It's only Mrs. Sharpe again." With this statement, the warden gave the dreaded signal and the trap doors on the gallows sprang open dropping Charles Sharpe and James McDonnell to their fate, while their stay of execution was just outside the jail door. When the warden finally unbolted the door, Mrs. Sharpe burst into the prison and up the stairs screaming, "I'm too late, I'm too late."

May 14, 2002
A young female guide was sitting in the cell block when something touched her leg. She smacked it to go away. "It was like someone was pulling on my pant leg — except there was nothing near me."

July 12, 2003
Jeanine, a longtime tour guide, had a young boy on a tour who heard a loud humming and talking coming from Cell 24. His sister saw a

flash of light in one of the cells, even though there was nothing there to flash or reflect any light and nothing to make a humming sound.

July 2004
EHK had previously written to us about her father's repeated and unsuccessful attempts at trying to remove the handprint by chiseling it out and replastering the wall of Cell 17. EHK now had come with a friend to tour the jail. Although we never open Cell 17 to the public, Tom relented and decided to make an exception because of the personal connection EHK had with the mysterious handprint. He opened Cell 17 and took her and her friend inside for a better look.

EHK was extremely grateful to get a close-up view of the handprint she had heard so much about but had never seen. Her friend, although skeptical of the handprint story, took several pictures inside Cell 17. Tom took some pictures of the women as well. A few weeks later, we received a letter from the skeptical friend saying that none of her photographs from Cell 17 had come out—the roll was blank. She was calling to ask Tom to send some of the photos he had taken. Tom gladly sent duplicates to the two women.

July 2004
A man was standing outside Cell 17 when he heard a voice from inside talking to him. He heard the voice proclaimed, "My name is Doyle and that's my handprint."

August 12, 2004
While on Bridget's tour, a woman about 35 years old suddenly jumped up and ran out of the cell block into the gift shop. She was crying and needed to go outside because she was completely overwhelmed by the sadness and despair in the building. Still crying, the woman admitted she was very embarrassed because she never before had lost control of her emotions like this. She said she could not go into the dungeon at all because something heavy had been pressing on her chest. Her young daughter, who had stayed on the tour, had no unusual feelings at all.

August 2004
Coming all the way from Iowa, Jackie and her husband
spent a bit of time chatting with us and walking around
the Old Jail. She later wrote us:

"Upon entering the first cell I felt anger, bad,
mean violent vibrations. I was very uncomfortable and broke out into an immediate sweat. It
was all I could do not to run. I had even
started to hyperventilate. My husband felt a
hand brush his hand as he entered and thought
it was you [Tom] passing him going into the
cell. But, when he turned around, you had not
even entered. No one was near him.

You then asked if I would be willing to go into
the second chamber [cell]. I was hesitant but
agreed to do it. Upon walking in, I felt com-
forted and cool. I could hear a faint voice
humming a lullaby-type song to my left. Very
loving and caring feelings surrounded me like a
gentle embrace. Check out the pictures and you
can see how strong the orb in this one is. What
an amazing difference between these two
chambers."

~ Jackie

Eager Listeners: *While Tara tells visitors about the Molly Maguires, at least six orbs can be seen floating overhead.*

August 31, 2004

A 10-year-old girl from Allentown, PA, was sitting in front of the gallows when someone kicked her leg. Annoyed, she turned to see who had kicked her, but found no one there. Her cousin, who was also on the tour, insisted her that she hadn't kicked her.

May 28, 2005

"The camera wouldn't work," mentioned a very surprised 35-year-old woman from Tamaqua, PA. She had just put new film in her camera but when she tried to take pictures the camera wouldn't work. "After I found my camera malfunctioning, I realized that I had felt creepy chills throughout the whole building."

June 2005

Twice during the lecture on the Molly Maguires a young man with a good view of Cell 17 heard short scratching noises. He discerned that the sounds were coming from Cell 17, and said he had heard and located these noises even before the guide related the mystery of the handprint in that cell.

June 21, 2005

"We came up from Blue Bell, PA, for a fun tour of the Old Jail," said K. & J. "As I was standing outside a jail cell I heard a noise behind me coming from the cell. Only thing is, the cell was empty and there was no one near me or near the cell to make the noise."

September 5, 2005

"As I was going down the steps into the women's cells, I felt something grab my upper left leg, just above my knee. I was startled and looked behind me, but there was no one there! It gave me such a chill," said L.H., a woman in her mid-30s from Upper Darby, PA.

September 10, 2005

As a woman from Reiglesville, PA, was walking through the cell block describing what she felt at each cell she abruptly stopped across from Cell 17 and said, "Oh, by the way, the handprint belongs to Mickey Doyle," and kept on walking.

September 17, 2005

A 27-year-old came to guide Lauren and told her she had come to the jail on a previous tour and had taken pictures in the cell block. Much to her surprise she found something unexpected when she looked at the pictures; in the picture of the last cell were two faces including one of a man with a beard and a hat.

October 2, 2005

The group was listening intently to Kayla tell the story of the trials and hangings of the Molly Maguires when suddenly a man interrupted. "You're wrong. That's not Campbell's handprint. It's

Doyle's handprint—Michael Doyle." Being a new guide, she did not know what to do when interrupted and didn't ask the man for more information.

While talking later with our guides, we realized that this was the fourth time someone had told us the handprint belonged to Michael Doyle. None of these people gave us any evidence or an explanation as to why he or she believed the handprint belonged to Michael Doyle. Each time it was simply made as a statement of fact.

So now the mystery increases: Some historians and authors believe the handprint is that of Alexander Campbell who was hanged in the jail in 1877; others say it is the print of Thomas P. Fisher, who was hanged in 1878; and now four separate people, who have no knowledge of each other, have told us it is the mark of Michael Doyle who was hanged along with Alexander Campbell in 1877. All three of these men had declared their innocence before each of their hangings. Moreover, no one that we are aware of has ever claimed that the handprint belonged to anyone other than one of these three men.

If there is a spirit in Cell 17? Who is it? Alexander Campbell? Thomas P. Fisher? Michael Doyle? Maybe someone, someday will come with some evidence or proof and help unravel the mystery of the ownership of the handprint on the wall of Cell 17.

October 19, 2005

Melissa, a young girl about 12 years old, was listening to the stories on the Ghost Tour. She was standing in front of her older friend who had her arms wrapped around her. Suddenly, Melissa felt someone pushing on her back as if someone or something was in between her and her friend. Her friend also felt this same force pushing on her stomach as she stood with her arms around Melissa.

Empty Gallows: *A mannequin once stood below these swaying nooses. But it was removed after a number of visitors reported that the "spirits were unhappy" with the mannequin standing on the gallows.*

October 29, 2005

After taking the Ghost Tour a couple felt they had to call us to tell us of their experience: As the wife was going into the cell block with the group she felt a terrible tightness and a fierce heat began building in her chest. Once it subsided she didn't think much about it. As she walked around the dungeon the same tightness and heat came over her again and then it went away. While driving the half-hour to their motel, she felt her chest on fire again. Although she didn't have a cold, she began coughing terribly and couldn't stop. These feelings lasted for about 15 minutes and then they subsided, this time for good.

October 2005

After touring the jail with Bridget, SF shared his feelings:

"I felt and saw an apparition of a man who was about 6 feet tall. He followed me through the tour. He whispered that he was innocent and he was not the only one. He told me there were countless mistrials and innocent men who were killed in this jail. I felt both of his hands on my shoulders. When we entered the dungeon he let go of me. He was frightened and refused to go inside the dungeon.

Once I checked out the dungeon and left, he grabbed both of my shoulders again. He told me again he was innocent and as we entered the hanging room he grew angry. He told me he despised the dummy that is on the gallows because a lot of innocent men died by hanging. He pleaded that the dummy should be taken off (of the gallows) because it is a mockery to those innocent men who have died.

He told me if I wanted to see the real men who died I should take a picture of each individual noose and then I could see them. My wife took a picture of the hangman display and two orbs showed up on the picture. Also, a document that I touched had a cold, electric, eerie sensation. It ended up being Alexander Campbell's guilty sentence."

Along for the Tour: *Orbs surround Tom and members of the Tamaqua Paranormal Research Society: From left: Paul, Tom, Jeff and Larry.*

October 29, 2005

A young woman about 30 years old and two friends came for the Ghost Tour. She wanted to talk with me and I noticed that she had a piece of black material draped over her arm and she gestured to it as she spoke. Because of the large number of people in the gift shop I could not talk with her but told her to be sure to stop and see me after her tour. About an hour later, she came back to show me the piece of clothing she had with her.

She said her sister had been on the Ghost Tour two weeks ago and had worn a white, long sleeved blouse and a black knit overblouse. They went from the jail directly to the restaurant and it was then that someone noticed the sister's overblouse was ripped in several places.

The young woman showed the black blouse to me and I saw that it was jaggedly ripped on one side from the hem to under the arm. It was also torn in several other areas on the opposite side and one sleeve was shredded at the hem. The woman said her sister had not felt anything near her and did not feel anything pull at her while on the tour. She emphasized that the group had gone from the tour directly to the restaurant so the blouse could not have been torn anywhere else. She knew it was hard to believe, but her sister said she could not find any explanation for what had happened to her blouse except that it had been torn by something or someone while in the Old Jail.

October 29, 2005

"As I was standing in the cell block," said a woman about 24 years old, "I saw a person on the walkway up above walk into a darkened cell. Only trouble was, there was no one up there and the cell doors were locked." She continued, "As I walked around I felt someone was playing with my hair and then I felt a pressure pushing on my leg."

Chapter 4

Balcony of the Unexplained

The Upper Cell Block

T he visitor's senses are startled when entering the cell block and encountering the beautiful ornamental cast iron staircase with hand-split oak railings. It's seemingly much too elegant for a jail. Located directly inside the front entrance to the cell block, the staircase was made in 1869 by Albright & Stroh of old Mauch Chunk. The ornamental ironwork railing, formed of gracefully patterned white cast iron, runs

Hand-Craftsmanship: *The 1869 white cast iron staircase with hand-split oak railings leads to the fourteen second floor cells.*

Perimeter of Iron: *The banister from the cast iron staircase continues around the balcony on the second floor of the cell block.*

around the perimeter of the entire cell block enclosing the balcony walkway. The 14 second floor cells open off this walkway.

Ascending the steep stairs the visitor might think of the sad and lonely men who, in the distant past, had walked up these steps knowing they would remain in this jail for many years. Off to the right is the library, a cell that was not used to house prisoners, but instead contains shelves for an assortment of books. More recently this room served a dual purpose and was utilized as a weight room as well as the library. The eyes are then drawn past the cells, which line the walls, each opening onto a balcony with a beautiful cast iron railing. At the end of the cell block stands the imposing gallows. To the left of the gallows is Cell 6, reported to once have been occupied by Thomas P. Fisher, the alleged Molly Maguire who worked to bring relief and equitable pay to the miners and who was accused of murder and hanged in the jail in 1878.

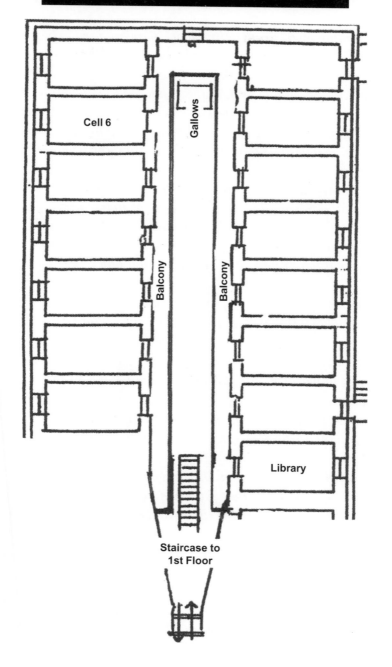

Second Floor Cell Block

Cell 6

Gallows

Balcony

Balcony

Library

Staircase to
1st Floor

~ Tales From the Upper Cell Block ~

May 1995

I was standing by the front door when a man I judged to be about 70 years old stopped me. This was the first time I was to hear this question: "Pardon me, but am I the only one who can't walk in certain places in this building?" I had no idea what the man meant. He explained that he had been walking on the second floor around the cell block and realized his breathing had changed and he felt dizzy and light-headed. He thought it might have been the air so he continued to walk around the cell block, returning to this same area three more times, all the while staying back from the second floor railing so as not to get dizzy by looking down. Each time he walked around that same place he felt dizzy and could not breathe. Since this was the first time I had heard such a tale, I had no idea what to tell him.

When we later discussed this man's report, I realized that I, too, had experienced something strange that day. When I was leading a group of visitors into the cell block I thought I saw my husband out of the corner of my eye. I was startled and thought, "Why in the world is Tom up there? That's not on the tour!" When I looked directly at the spot, I saw no one standing there. For my next three tours, whenever I entered the cell block I continued to think I saw someone standing in this same spot.

The place where I had glimpsed someone—someone who wasn't actually there—was the same place where the man had difficulty breathing. This spot was directly in front of a cell where Thomas P. Fisher, one of the Molly Maguires, was confined and directly above the spot where seven of the Molly Maguires met their sad fate on the gallows.

June 1995

"I have chills up and down my spine," whispered a Scranton, PA, man who had just walked around the back of the cell block. He

Hot Spot: *Many visitors report unusual experiences in and around Cell 6, the cell with the open iron door.*

had experienced a chilling effect directly above the area where the Irish miners had been hanged. *Little did we know in 1995 that reports of chills were to be repeated many times over in the years to come—and all without explanation!*

August 1995
As a forty-something husband and wife toured the jail together, the wife felt chills as she passed the library and also felt "a chilly, strange feeling" at the left rear side of the second floor.

August 1995
Although the cell block was warm, it was not hot enough to cause sweating. Yet the woman in the Harley Davidson t-shirt was wide-eyed and sweating profusely as she came down the stairs. She had a "very strange and heavy feeling" and was anxious to return to her room at the Inn of Jim Thorpe. Meanwhile, on the second floor, another woman was experiencing shortness of breath and other unusual feelings.

August 1995
"I had the feeling of someone being on the second floor of the cell block to the right of the window. Talking about it gives me goose bumps and chills. It was not a feeling of anyone going to cause hurt to anyone, just a feeling of something or someone there."

— Marilyn, New York.

August 8, 1995
"I felt a hand on my shoulder during the entire tour and when I went to the back left area of the second floor, there was a very strong feeling as if something was there." These were the words of a woman as she celebrated her 21st birthday by touring the jail.

August 14, 1995
A woman about 45 years of age, wearing a purple outfit, toured the building with guide, Amanda. Afterwards Amanda mentioned to Tom that the woman had felt a "heavy presence" in the dungeon and asked Tom to talk with her. The woman was still quite shaken and said she felt as if heavy hands had been pushing down on her shoulders. Once she was calm, Tom suggested she walk around some more and then come back to chat with him again.

Joined by her husband, the woman made her way to the second floor of the cell block. Tom was standing by the shower room, and two teenage guides, Liz and Amanda, were standing by the bottom of the wrought-iron staircase watching. Suddenly, all three were startled by a shuffle, and Liz saw the woman stumble backwards shaking violently. The woman had attempted to walk into the second-floor library, was pushed backwards with a great force, seemed almost to faint and was, luckily, caught by her husband.

Tom then noticed our own guides were quite shaken; Amanda was white with fear and clutching her arms, while Liz was red-faced and very distraught.

Tom rushed upstairs to help our visitor and noticed that the woman's facial muscles were still quivering. He offered her a chair, which she refused, and then assisted her back down the stairs with her bewildered husband following. The woman hurried through the gift shop and dashed out the front door, almost leaping down the front steps.

In the years that Amanda worked as a guide, an overwhelming number of people from her tours reported odd happenings. Although Amanda never experienced anything odd herself, we have been told that some people can act as a channeler for spirits without ever knowing it.

August 20, 1995
This was to be the day Cell 6 demanded attention:

"Strange chills and goose bumps on my arms" is how two 30-year-old men described their feelings around Cell 6.

Later on in the day, two teenage boys told us they had felt strange chills causing the hair on the backs of their necks to stand up when they walked past Cell 6.

After completing her tour, a woman about 25 years old walked around the Old Jail just looking in the cells and reading the signs. She also felt strange emotions in the area of Cell 6.

September 1995
As Bridget, a tour guide, walked around the second floor area above the site of the hanging, she walked full force into a wall of air in the area of Cell 6. She could not walk any further or get through "the wall" so she had to turn around and walk in the op-

posite direction. In three years of giving tours, this was the first time Bridget had ever experienced the feeling of "walking into a wall" that was not there.

September 1995
A waitress brought her daughter for a tour but changed her mind and decided to wait outside while her daughter took the tour. The mother's hesitancy was bolstered when her daughter told her that as she walked around the back of the second floor she walked right into a wall of air and could not get past it. She also experienced breathing problems in the library on the second floor.

September 9, 1995
Barbara from Philadelphia, PA, returned the day after her tour to tell us of her strange experience in the building: She wanted to feel what a prisoner must feel when locked in a cell, so she asked her husband to shut her inside Cell 6. When she was halfway inside she had to stop because the floor of the cell was "sloped" and she could not walk up the slope to the back of the cell. Surprised and disappointed, she stepped back into the hallway to tell her husband to check out the terribly odd, slanted floor. He looked into the cell and couldn't understand what his wife was talking about, so he went into the cell to look around. When he came out he told her that the floor was absolutely flat.

September 9, 1995
"I couldn't walk back there—the far back end of the second floor cell block," said a woman with dark hair who also couldn't walk around the corner to Cell 6. " I had such weird feelings. "

July 1996
A woman started to go into the library but suddenly fell backwards into her surprised husband's arms. She explained to her confused husband that as she had entered the door, a strong force had pushed against her and forced her backwards. *Authors' note: We had heard a very similar report during the previous summer.*

The Famous Library: *This cell at the top of the stairs makes an appearance in many of our tales: from books moving, to women getting pushed, to girls being kicked, the cell seems to be the home to more than just books.*

July 1996

The evening after the woman related the now familiar story of being pushed from the library, Tom went up to the library to "have a talk" with whatever or whomever was there. Never having given much thought to ghosts, he tongue-in-cheek demanded that there be no more nonsense and if the disturbances continued he would have a priest come and bless the building. When he came home that night he told me he had felt really silly talking to the walls of an empty room.

July 1996 (two days after the above "lecture ")

I was selling admission tickets at the sales desk when a woman about 35 years old came to me and in an undertone said she wanted to tell me something. I thought, oh no, what happened now. She asked if there had ever been any problems in the building, especially in the area of the library. I hoped she wasn't going to tell me that she had been pushed. What she told me really surprised me! She said she had gone into the library to look at it. As she entered, she felt a "feeling of peace" descend upon her unlike anything she had experienced before and it was the most peaceful feeling she had ever experienced.

Several months later we heard another rendition of this story. An older woman related to us that this was her second visit to the Old Jail. On her first visit she had found that she could not step foot in the library. A "very foreboding presence" was keeping her from entering the room. When she returned home it frustrating her that she was unable to enter this small room and promised herself she had to return to try it again. Now on her second visit, she had made her way hesitantly to the second floor library. She told us she was flabbergasted by what she found. Not only did she have no trouble, whatsoever, in entering the room, but now she found that this room had the most peaceful aura of any room in the jail.

July 7, 1996

After being overwhelmed with sudden, terrible chills in the dungeon, a 12-year-old girl said she had the same feelings on the second floor of the cell block while she was looking down at the gallows. Tom said it was alright if she and her father wanted to go back into the cell block. But as soon as the young girl reached the top of the stairs she exclaimed, "I'm scared!" Rodney and Liz, both guides, watched as the girl hurried to the front door, followed by her very bewildered father.

July 8, 1996

The 12-year-old girl from yesterday returned with her family for another visit. After her tour, the young girl was asked, "Well, how did it go today." She was very reluctant to talk about her feelings today, but finally admitted that she had felt someone was walking next to her with a hand on her shoulder or behind her neck, such as a companion would do. Surprisingly, the young girl was not a bit afraid, just reluctant to talk about it.

Kate's Orb: *Guide Kate and visitor Steve are unaware that they have been joined by an orb.*

August 1996

The increasingly large number of people telling us about their baffling experiences in the library had alarmed us. It was a difficult decision, but we decided to close the library by putting a "Do Not Enter" sign across the door. Hopefully, this would lessen any disturbance resulting from people entering this room.

August 8, 1996

A woman with black hair had very strange and uncomfortable feelings at the back of the second floor cell block and could not walk around the corner to the back. She did not know why she couldn't walk there, only that her feet simply would not move.

1997

After working as a guide for a while, Cathy realized that every time she went up the stairs to the second floor of the cell block it seemed as if her heart raced. One day she decided to check this out more thoroughly. She began by taking her pulse in the cell block, then monitored her pulse as she slowly walked up the stairs.

Local Craftsmanship: *The cast iron railing was forged in 1869 by Albright & Strohl of Mauch Chunk, now Jim Thorpe.*

She noticed her pulse actually beat faster as she neared the top of the stairs. Another guide was watching her and added that Cathy's eyes dilated as she reached the second floor and constricted when she returned to the cell block floor.

August 1998
"I felt like I was going to have a heart attack!" exclaimed a man who had just walked around the back of the second floor of the cell block. "My heart just kept beating faster and faster."

September 12, 1998
Two people walked around the second floor of the cell block and finally stopped in the library. As they stood inside, they noticed a Bible move and drop several inches. The man quickly left the building because he felt a "rush of terrible chills."

September 27, 1998
"I sensed a freaky feeling on the left side of the second floor about

one-half way down to the back. I was overcome with the shakes and had to sit down in a hurry," related one visitor.

March 1999
Shortly after St. Patrick's Day we heard from a neighbor that she had experienced something very odd. Late one night as she was passing the jail she heard music coming from the jail and turned to analyze the shadows by the front door. She was able to make out the shape of a man playing the bagpipes and listened as the sorrowful tune came wafting down the street. She quickly hurried home to inform her family she had seen a ghost. Not being surprised anymore by unusual tales we recorded this one with all the rest.

Several months later we were reminded of this story. Following his tour a man confessed to us that he had been here before. He had been driving through town late one night when he passed the jail. Overcome with sorrow for the Molly Maguires he decided to stop to pay tribute to them. So, at midnight, he offered to the Molly Maguires (and to an unwitting neighbor) a solo on his pipes.

September 21, 1999
"My legs felt exceptionally heavy and unable to move fast when I went by the library," said Edna, "I also had a strong feeling in that area that the spirits in the library want to be left completely alone."

June 2001
Rick was surprised by the feeling of oppressiveness he experienced around Cell 25. "It was like the room was closing in around me."

July 2001
We decided to reopen the library to visitors. It was apparent that people were still entering the library even though a "Do Not Enter" sign was posted at the doorway because visitors continued to report strange happenings in this room.

August 2001
Jessica, a 12-year-old girl from Cleveland, OH, spent some time walking around the building after her tour. She had funny feelings all over the building, and we suggested she return later in the day when most of the visitors would be gone so she could spend additional time in a quiet building. She returned later that day and we accompanied her around the cell block. After she went into the library, we heard Jessica speaking and realized she was carrying on a conversation with someone, but we also knew there was no one except her in that room. She came out of the library and told us that she indeed was not alone in the library because she could feel somebody repeatedly kicking the back of her knee. She said she had tried asking questions but received no response until she raised her hands and told the spirit to push her fingers— right hand for "yes", left hand for "no."

To our astonishment Jessica told us that her fingers had been pushed in answer to her questions. He didn't answer all of them but she had learned that he was a man in his 30s. At this point our daughter, Kathleen, hesitantly, yet curiously, joined the girl as she re-entered the library. After a moment, Jessica looked puzzled and slowly turned to Kathleen to apologetically explain that he would only communicate with her if she were alone.

Kathleen retreated back to the hallway and listened as Jessica successfully continued her questions. She came back out of the room to tell us that whoever was in there did not seem to know he was dead. She returned to the library and we could hear her telling him that he was dead and that it was OK for him to" leave and go home."

This young girl did not seem to be the least bit frightened or embarrassed about carrying on a conversation in an empty room. She later related to us that when she recalled this conversation with an unseen person it made her feel "very strange." After that occurrence we checked on the activities in that cell on a regular basis and noticed a dramatic decline in unusual activity, feelings, and emotions.

August 2001
Ian and several other guides decided to take Polaroid pictures in the library. One picture showed Ian standing alone in the middle of the library, directly under the overhead light. When we looked closely at the picture, what a surprise! Yellow areas shaped very much like mysterious hands could be seen on each of Ian's shoulders.

Rope of Death: A noose sways from the recreated gallows.

September 30, 2001
A young man lingered after his tour and made his way to the left side of the upper cell block. He explained that he could "sense a spirit in Cell 6" and that he had felt "strange vibrations" in the area just above the gallows.

July 22, 2002
"I went into the library to see what it was like in there," a young female guide told us. "When I went in the back, it got very warm. When I came out I walked all the way around upstairs and felt someone shake me. I heard a person plop down on something when I was standing by the rail and then someone touched my cross necklace. I came downstairs really fast."

Summer 2002

"We were closing up the jail for the night while Mr. McBride was outside working. We went through our usual routine: to make sure everyone was out of the building we went from room to room calling out, "Hello," expecting, of course, not to get an answer. Ian went into the Visitors' Room to make sure no one was there, while I hollered up the stairs, "Hello! We're closing up. Hello". Suddenly we heard a little girl upstairs answer, "Hi!"

Then we heard footsteps upstairs, like running feet, and children giggling. Since we thought there might be children hiding upstairs, we went up to look around. Ian and I looked in every room but we couldn't find anyone.

We were going downstairs to tell Mr. McBride what happened because we didn't want to be responsible for locking anyone inside the jail. When we were heading towards the door, I felt like we were being followed. Ian obviously felt this, too, because we turned around at the same time. There was no one there—the hallway and the stairs were completely empty. The door out of the building was directly in front of us, so we made a mad dash to get outside!"

— Matt

June 3, 2004
After experiencing various unsettling feelings in the dungeon, a 20-year-old woman returned to the library. She felt her heart beat as if she were having a heart attack and could only stay a short while. She had also felt violence in the center cell area in the woman's cells. Tom told her that a psychic had toured the jail and had felt a woman had been raped in this cell. The young woman disagreed, saying she only felt the sensation of a death, not rape. "There are restless spirits roaming around who want to be freed," is how she described her impressions. She told us that "in order to let these spirits free" we must reopen the doorway that once connected the women's cells with the main cell block, which had been sealed more than seventy years ago.

June 22, 2004
A 10-year-old girl from Maryland approached her guide, Bridget, to say she was sensitive to spirits and wasn't afraid of them. While she was in the library her right arm had become cold. And while she was in the dungeon she had felt a great, heavy pressure on her shoulder.

September 10, 2004
A middle-aged woman had experienced strange feelings during her tour, so Tom told her she was welcome to walk around the building for a while. She later found Tom to tell him that she had felt a cold sensation and the hair on the back of her neck was standing up while she was in the cell block and also on the second floor near Cell 9. As she had walked through the dungeon she had felt an extreme heaviness descend on the back of her shoulders as if it were the "pressure of doom."

September 26, 2004
A "strong presence" made itself known to a man about 27 years old as he walked around on the second floor of the cell block . He told guide Bridget that this feeling was especially strong in the area just above the gallows.

October 12, 2004
"A fist pushing down on my chest and stomach" is how a young boy described what he felt as he entered the library. He had felt strange and unusual emotions and feelings elsewhere in the jail as well. Although his older brother had also felt uncomfortable, his feelings were not as strong. Their parents smiled at their tales, but offered no reaction or explanation.

2005
One day our guides were talking about the difficulty each one of them had breathing and speaking when they would take visitors up to the Warden's Bedroom on the second floor. "Boy, I can't talk when I get up there, can you?" "Do you have trouble breathing in that bedroom?" "Wonder what's up with that bedroom because I can't keep on talking up there." I realized I, too, was out of breath during this part of the tour, but I had simply attributed it to having just climbed a long flight of stairs and being older than our teenage guides. We have no idea why this shortness of breath happens in this bedroom area, but it happens to each of our guides on a regular basis.

June 20, 2005
Several people from different tours, two woman about 22 and 32, a boy about 13, and a girl about 8 years old, all stopped to tell us of their unusual experiences. Each felt a heavy presence near Cell 6 above the gallows. The 32-year-old woman could not breath and was unable to walk past the area, and the 22-year-old woman felt the presence of sadness and evil by and below this cell.

July 2005
"Dad, someone pushed me up in the library! Someone REALLY pushed me," a 10-year-old boy interrupted his father's conversation with Tom. After the father had dismissed his son's remarks and the son had walked away, Tom quietly explained that others had reported very similar sensations in the area his son felt he had been pushed.

Old Jail Guides
Through the Years

Jeanine, Alicia &
Bridget '97

Tom & Chelsey '05

Lauren '05

Erin & Jessie (standing)
Heather & Jeanine '02

Matt '03

Liz '95

Steve '99

Alisa, Trisha & Tara '04

Ian, Chad & Jeanine '99

~ 69 ~

August 20, 2005
A handsome man, about 45 years old with dark hair, had some unusual feelings during his tour. "Goosebumps all over and tingles up his spine" made him feel "creepy" as he stood in front of Cell 18 near the gallows.

August 20, 2005
"It sounded like shoes sliding across a floor," is how a Robin, a young mother of three children, described the shuffling sound she heard in Cell 7 (the last cell on the left side of the upper cell block.) Because the whole cell block was very quiet at the time, the sound was quite distinct. This artist from Hilltop, PA looked around and saw no one in or near the cell.

September 24, 2005
"I walked into Cell 6 and felt an eerie feeling. I'm not quite sure what I felt, but I could tell that something just didn't feel quite right," said NAW of Lansdale, PA.

October 2005
"I was walking slowly up on the second floor of the cell block. I walked towards the back when suddenly, just outside Cell 6, I heard a door slam shut behind me. I jumped and spun around only to find there was no door behind me to close," nervously explained a man who had just finished the Ghost Tour.

October 8, 2005
A mother, about 40 years old, and her 13-year-old son had previously visited the jail shortly after it had opened in 1995 when the son was only 3 years old. The mother said the little boy had quietly wandered in and out of all the cells. But when he entered the library he started screaming and carrying on. As she tried to comfort him he said he did not like being in there. Now a decade later, he felt nothing unusual during his tour but said he still remembers the unusual feelings from his first visit.

Tight Spaces: Cell doors were designed so prisoners would have to duck when entering the 8'x13' cell that was shared with 1-3 other prisoners.

October 15, 2005

Elizabeth, a young girl from Jim Thorpe, was visiting the jail with her grandmother. "When I was up on the second floor of the cell block walking around the balcony and the library I could not get my breath. It was awful. I couldn't breath. As I walked around up there I felt like somebody was watching me and I decided I just had to get out. I also felt like something kicked at my ankle."

October 26, 2005

As a group of Northwest Area High School students were finishing their school tour, I noticed them all gathering around one young girl about 12 or 13 years old. I asked what they were all excited about and they told the girl to tell me her story. She said she was walking up the stairs to the second floor of the cell block when her necklace began to dig into her skin around her neck. Her class-mates suggested she go up the stairs again and she did, walking very slowly—only to come hurrying down saying her necklace was again digging into her skin. I noticed that the skin around her neck was indeed very red and she was visibly upset. Then I looked at the necklace—it contained nothing sharp. It was simply a typi-cal teenager's modern necklace of beads shaped like flat stars or flowers connected by several small, round beads.

October 29, 2005

While visiting the jail with their families, three teenage girls were busily visiting all of the cells with a tape recorder in hand. As they went into one of the second floor cells, one of the girls felt sick and nauseous. A woman with them asked, "Do you want to go down?" They then decided to leave the jail. Once back in their hotel room, they listened to their recording and near the end of the tape they heard the woman ask "Do you want to go down?" Then they heard a man's slow, rough voice say, "Wait, don't go down!" There was no man with them nor any man nearby to hear the woman's question to the girl and none of them had heard the man while they were in the jail. They were all so excited about hearing the voice on their recording that they made a special trip back to the jail the next day to tell us what they had heard.

~ Chapter 5 ~

Chamber
of the Dark

The Dungeon

D ark . . . Dreary . . . Dismal . . . The word "dungeon" conjures many images, and the dungeon in the Old Jail does not disappoint. A stairway at the back of the main cell block leads down to the dungeon and seemingly back a few hundred years in time. A heavy feeling of despair and doom emanates from all around.

The dark dungeon hallway leads into even darker cells. With no electricity in any cell, darkness enveloped the prisoners day and night. Eight of the 16 cells originally had sheet iron doors and were most likely used for solitary confinement. The temperature in the cells was unstable because the door had only several 1" diameter holes and a 5" square opening for air, food and light, which filtered though from dim lanterns in the hallway. Daylight was limited in each cell by an iron covering on the very small window.

The dungeon cells are much more primitive than the cells upstairs in the main cell block. The sanitary facilities originally consisted of the commonly used "slop buckets" of the olden days. However, in the early 1900s, one "modern" toilet was installed in one cell. Because of this one amenity, this cell has been dubbed the "luxury cell" by our guides, and this is the cell that visitors enter as part of their tour.

The dungeon was the "jail's jail," as one former guard called it. No records were kept as to how many prisoners were incarcerated, how long prisoners were confined or what methods of punishment were incorporated in these desolate cells. But reports do indicate that at one time prisoners were restrained with shackles. Although we have no records of what may have transpired in this harsh and forbidding place, imagination and history lead the mind onto many terrible paths. In 1979 Judge John Lavelle officially closed the dungeon thus ending the confinement of prisoners in the "jail's jail."

~ The Dungeon & the Molly Maguires ~

Two alleged Molly Maguires, James (Jimmy) Kerrigan and Edward Kelly, both accused of the 1875 murder of coal mine boss John P. Jones were confined in the Mauch Chunk prison, now the Old Jail. Jimmy Kerrigan was a prisoner for more than 19 months with some of this time spent locked in solitary confinement in the dungeon. It is not known in which cells these men were held.

While in the dungeon, Kerrigan received several visits from Gen. Charles Albright, who was the prosecutor in the Molly Maguire trials and also an attorney for the Lehigh and Wilkes-Barre Coal Company. After Kerrigan turned states evidence and agreed to testify against his friends he was moved from the dungeon's solitary confinement up to a cell in the main cell block. As a prisoner Kerrigan received numerous gratuities including cigars, bananas and hair oil. During his confinement the coal company granted his wife open credit for purchases at the coal company store. Because of Kerrigan's testimony, many coal miners were hanged.

On April 10,1877, the Carbon County Commissioners issued to Kerrigan and his wife a promissory note in the amount of $1,000 payable one year from that date. This payment was the equivalent of three years of miner's pay and translates into over $50,000 in today's wages. The minutes of this Carbon County Commissioners' meeting do not give the reason why the exceptionally large promissory note was granted. Interestingly, this note was given two months prior to the hanging of four convicted Molly Maguires and was payable ten months after the hangings were completed.

While Kerrigan was in the Mauch Chunk jail his trial dates in Schuylkill County were extended and eventually thrown out upon the petition of attorneys of the railroads and the coal companies.

Ultimately, Kerrigan and his family left Pennsylvania for Richmond, VA, where he assumed his wife's maiden name of Higgins. Many historians now feel that Kerrigan was paid for his testimony with gifts, money, and most importantly, freedom.

Edward Kelly, a very young man who did not testify against any of the other accused Molly Maguires, was held in the dungeon and was hanged in the jail on June 21, 1877, after being found guilty of the murder of the mine boss, John P. Jones.

~ Tales from the Dungeon ~

May 1995
To celebrate our grand opening, an open house for all local business owners was held in the Old Jail and many people wandered around the building after their escorted tours. As one local businessman approached the door to the dungeon he lunged backwards and almost fell. His explanation later was that he felt as if someone had hit him on the chest. He vowed never to enter that place again and, true to his word, has never returned.

July 1995
We were getting used to having people ask about the strange emotions and feelings that the jail seemed to evoke, but it still came as a surprise to find that a woman was sobbing while touring the dungeon and she had no idea why.

July 1995
Two women felt various strong emotions in different areas of the jail. One of the women felt extremely weak in the knees because she could feel the beatings, tortures and killings in the dungeon.

July 1995
A young actress and a friend spent a very long time walking around the building and taking in the feelings and emotions of the tragic events that happened so many years ago. She felt "extreme sadness, despair and anguish" throughout the building and while walking in and out of several cells in the dungeon. After entering one particular cell, she came out in a rush and hurried up the stairs practically running to the gift shop. She told us that as she stood in a cell she distinctly heard a voice say, "Get out of here!" She said she knew by the voice that it "meant business" and that she and her friend were not going to argue and they ran.

July 20, 1995
"Chills. I feel chills and a hand on my back," declared a 12-year-old girl. The young, redheaded girl accompanying her would not or could not go into the dungeon. Amanda, the guide, heard the girls say, "They're here," and noticed that they were both physically trembling.

August 1995
"I could see him in there," said Tom M. of Hazleton, PA, who was visiting with his wife. "We went into a cell in the dungeon and there was a man sitting in there with his leg cut off." Tom felt the man in the cell had cut off his own leg because it had become infected with gangrene.

Dungeon

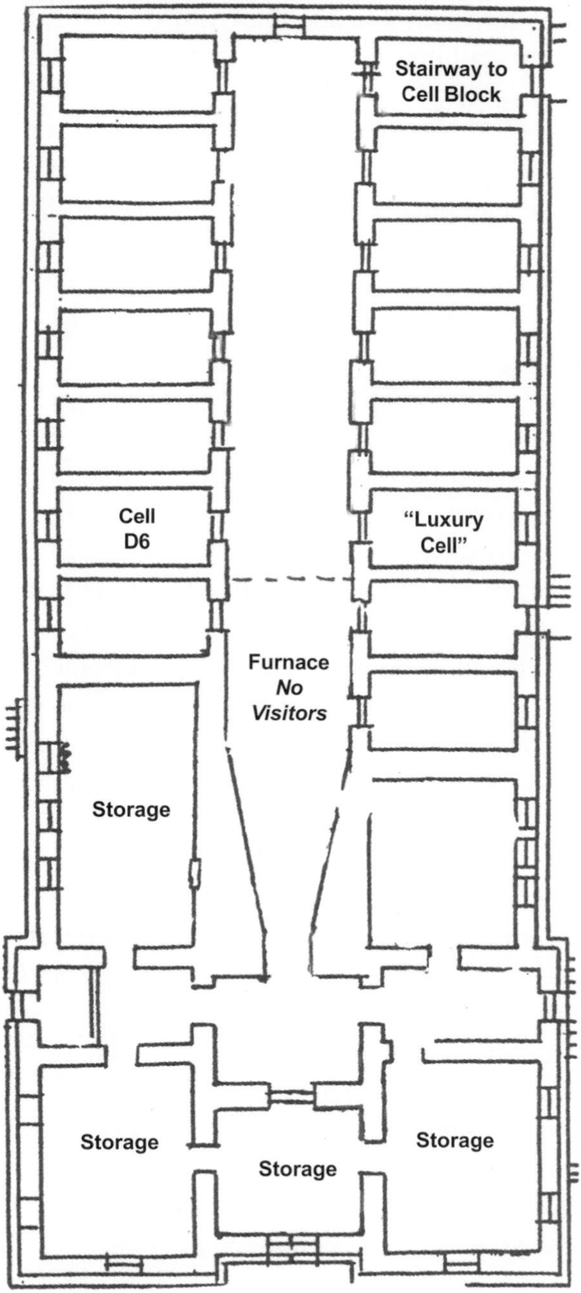

Stairway to
Cell Block

Cell
D6

"Luxury
Cell"

Furnace
*No
Visitors*

Storage

Storage

Storage

Storage

August 14, 1995
"A heavy presence," is how the woman in purple described her feeling in the dungeon. Earlier in the day this same woman had great difficulty walking up the staircase to the second floor.

October 1995
Guide Ed will never forget the day he was leading a tour into the dungeon when a Summit Hill, PA, woman suddenly whirled around and bolted past him up the stairs. "We had a TV cameraman on the tour and he was walking behind the tour group filming them as they walked around the building. As the group entered the dungeon door the woman stopped suddenly, spun around and nearly knocked the TV cameraman over in her rush to get up the steps and away from the dungeon. That night when we watched the news on TV, we saw the report on the Old Jail and saw the camera bobble as the woman ran into it."

Later the woman explained, "I felt like someone punched me in the chest with a fist. I couldn't breathe. I had just walked a few feet through the dungeon door when I began to feel very threatened. I couldn't go any further. I felt like someone was going to hurt me. I grabbed my friend's arm and told her I wanted to go home. I was still gasping for breath when I got outside."

July 1996
The door of one cell in the dungeon just won't stay closed. When we take visitors to the dungeon we stop to point out the details of the extremely heavy, 3/8" thick, iron door on one particular cell. In order for everyone on the tour to see it, the door has to be completely or, at least, partially closed. To their frustration our guides will often find this door wide open and will have to close it. When I again reminded our guides not to open this door, each claimed he or she did not open it. There is absolutely no draft or breeze in this area that would cause such a heavy door to open by itself and the door is level, yet it keeps opening.

Dank Dungeon: *The 16 dungeon cells open from a center hallway.*

July 7, 1996
As a 12 years old entered the dungeon, she complained of feeling very chilled. When asked if she was all right she said she was fine. As the group went into a cell, the young girl hung back hesitantly. She stopped, ran from the dungeon back up to the gift shop. The girl and her family asked if others had similar feelings and was assured that she was not the only one to feel uncomfortable in the building. She mentioned that she had felt similar chills on the second floor of the cell block when she had walked up there.

July 20, 1996
"Chills—very strange chills" were described by a young girl, about 12 or 13 years old, when she entered the dungeon.

July 1999
"A heaviness in the chest" and "tingling sensations" in his arms and shoulders made Tom wonder "what in the world was happening." As he walked in the dungeon, he experienced a strong urge to burst into tears near the cell at the far back left.

July 15, 1999
Dorrien felt very dizzy and unsteady in the dungeon around the

second cell on the left. Once she moved past this cell, the dizzy feeling suddenly disappeared. She walked into another cell, immediately turned around, hurried out of the dungeon and dashed up to the fresh air of the exercise yard.

When I talked with her outside, she said she left the cell in such a hurry because she had the feeling that whatever was in that cell wanted her out of there and so she ran. She also explained she had a strange sensation and a dizzy feeling on the second floor of the cell block. But when she walked towards the stairs the feeling disappeared and she, once again, felt fine.

August 1999
"The two cells in the dungeon have definite spirit energy in them," Debora Ann said. "I could sense a man pacing back and forth inside a cell and the soft weeping sounds of a woman or young man crying came from another cell, the 2nd or 3rd cell on the side opposite the dungeon door." She also detailed the many strange feelings she had felt on the second floor of the cell block.

October 1999
As a man and his friend pensively walked around the dungeon, he thought he heard something so he stopped to listen. Yes, he did hear something. It was a voice—but no one else was in the dungeon and his friend was not speaking to him. As he listened more closely, he realized the gruff voice from within a cell was saying, " Get the %#$@ out of here!" The man didn't argue and hastily left the dungeon, pulling his bewildered friend after him.

June 17, 2000
Scott was walking into the dungeon with his tour group when the lights went on and off with no one touching them.

June 20, 2000
"Angry spirits shouting," were the words a woman on Steve's tour used to describe the noises she had heard in the dungeon.

Dungeon Orbs:
Numerous sized orbs can be seen in the back of the dungeon.

August 2000

That same cell door is still opening by itself! This is the cell door that we show to our visitors so it must be kept closed. We reported in 1996 that this cell door refused to stay closed, and now, 4 years later, we have the same problem—a door that opens by itself.

October 13, 2001

While in the dungeon, a man and his young daughter were standing in the Cell D6. The daughter saw a man with a "droopy mustache and a beard" wearing a blue shirt. But when she told her dad to look at the man "who was watching her," they only found an empty cell.

July 2002

"Tell Mrs. McBride," I overheard one of our guides say to Ian, a teenage guide. When I asked what they were discussing and what he should tell me, Ian sheepishly said that something had happened in the dungeon: "I was walking across the dungeon toward the back after turning on the lights when I walked under the ceiling vent and saw a light coming down. I thought it was coming from the cell block through those little holes in the manhole cover. It flashed instead of just shining down. When this happened I got a really bad headache. I took another step or two and suddenly everything stopped, like when you pause a movie, and it kind of shifts. I suddenly felt a rush of air coming up from behind me on the left. It slid along my arm at my side. Then I saw a round shape like a tube, maybe four to five feet long, that passed by me and then turned back towards me. I then heard a voice from far away toward the right rear say in an angry, low voice, 'Hey, boy! What are you doing?' I did not answer. I just ran."

June 21, 2003
A young man and woman asked about spirits in the jail because they could sense their presence. The man had gotten goosebumps in the dungeon because he could feel a spirit there. He then become very sweaty and had to leave. Both these visitors had also felt a presence in the cell block behind the gallows.

August 24, 2003
Michael of Catasaqua, PA, told Ed that he saw a spirit standing in the middle of Cell D6 and he could sense "terrible anger" in the second cell from the end on the far side.

June 3, 2004
A woman about 20 and her companion stopped to mention that they felt some strange feelings in various places in the jail. The woman began to show me her photographs from the dungeon that she had just taken with her $400 camera/phone. When she looked at the pictures she was dismayed to see that most of the pictures taken throughout the jail were not in her camera! Only a few of the photos taken in the dungeon had come out. The couple asked to return to the dungeon to take some more pictures, but would not go unless Tom accompanied them. They photographed all the cells on the east side of the dungeon. As she began to enter a cell along the opposite wall, she suddenly stopped in her tracks and bellowed to her friend , "Do NOT go in there!" She offered no explanation, left the dungeon and went up to the library with her perplexed friend in tow. They only spent a very short time on the second floor where she explained to Tom that her heart was beating as if she were having a heart attack. They both seemed extremely anxious to leave.

Lights in the Dungeon: *The original dungeon cells had no lights; the light on the left was installed for our visitors' viewing. The light spot on the right was not present when the photo was taken, and there is nothing reflective near this cell door.*

June 19, 2004

A young woman returned to the jail for a repeat tour and stopped to tell us the unusual feelings she had experienced on her first tour. She was very sensitive to spirits and had felt many sensations in the jail. On that first tour, she had been standing in the back of the group in the center of the basement when she felt someone grab her skirt and then her shoulder. Annoyed, she turned to see who had been so rude and discovered that there was no one behind her. After the tour, she noticed her skirt was torn where she had felt it grabbed. Later, when she examined her shoulder, she found she had marks on it as if a hand had gripped it. Her second tour on June 19th was uneventful.

June 20, 2004

"I thought it was my father pushing me and I was mad," a 10-year-old told guide Tara. As the tour came up from the dungeon into the exercise yard, the girl felt someone push her from the back, as if to tell her to hurry up. She thought her father was behind her and that he was pushing her to hurry up the stairs. She turned around to tell him she couldn't go any faster, but there was no one behind her. Shocked, she realized that her father was two people in front of her and she was the last person coming up the stairs.

August 2004
Jackie and her husband visited from Iowa and later sent us many photos with visible orbs, which Jackie said she had read could be either spirits or angels.

> *August 2004*
> *"I really heard a voice say, 'So, how do you like our dungeon,' when were in the basement on the first tour. No one else heard it."*
> *~ Jackie*

September 11, 2004
A middle-aged woman (who said she was young-at-heart) was standing in the dungeon with her back to the furnace area while listening to guide Dan talk about the dungeon. She felt a slight shove on the right side of her back so she turned around to see who was pushing her. All she saw was a wall with peeling plaster, no one near her, there was not even enough room for someone to stand behind her.

Later that night, this same woman joined us for a rehearsal of our Ghost Tour. When this tour reached the dungeon, the woman looked closely at the spot where she had been standing when she felt someone shove her and where she had turned and seen the wall. She was unnerved to see there was no wall anywhere near where she had been standing. There was only open space.

September 11, 2004
Meanwhile, on this same tour, a middle-aged man heard a noise in his right ear. He stressed it was not speech or ringing, but he could hear it coming from Cell D6 "Air much colder than normal" then passed over his right arm coming from behind. It lasted about 15 seconds and then disappeared just as quickly as it had appeared.

September 11, 2004
Chris and Brooke were looking into the cells along the right side of the dungeon. When the flash of their camera went off they glimpsed a chair in the corner of the cell. Suddenly they smelled something "funny" and felt something touch them.

September 11, 2004
Jessica, a 25-year-old who liked ghost stories, told us the following: "I was with a group in the dungeon. After the tour we were allowed to take pictures so I was taking the last picture. I asked my sister-in-law if she was fine and she answered "yes." Just after I asked her she walked away and I heard a moan with heavy breathing in my right ear. I thought it was the wind and I was going to walk away, but then I felt someone poke me in the back, meaning to get out! We left immediately."

September 20, 2004
An older woman was very perplexed and concerned because while she was on her tour in the dungeon, standing apart from the group, she had felt hands pushing down on her back.

September 26, 2004
"I felt two strong presences in the dungeon, one sad and another malignant. I didn't feel any physical pushes or pulls, but some electric static energy moved about me," related a man in his 20s from Flushing, NY.

October 2004
Here we go again! For 10 years the same cell door keeps open-

Round Orbs & Vents:
The holes in the ceiling are vents that originally conducted heat up to the first and second floor cells.

ing by itself. We close the iron door to show our visitors and when we return it's open. Could it be that something in that cell simply doesn't want to be confined?

October 2004

Dan, one of our guides, went down into the dungeon with a camera with new batteries and planned on taking lots of photographs. As he began taking pictures, his batteries went dead.

A pattern we had been noticing was now increasing dramatically. Over the years, people have asked if our gift shop carried batteries because their new batteries had died. They told us they would attempt to take pictures with a camera with new batteries and after perhaps one or two pictures, the batteries stopped working. No batteries, no camera, no photographs! It doesn't seem to matter whether the cameras are digital or film.

October 23, 2004

"Come quick," a guide shouted at me during the Ghost Tour. "A man just fell down in the dungeon." I panicked as I ran. I was afraid to find out what happened. I kept thinking, "What do I do if this man has had a heart attack?"

However, the young man and his friend were already on their way up when Tom and I met them. He was a handsome man, quite tall, wearing a long, leather coat. We all went to sit in the kitchen so he could catch his breath and tell us what had happened. We were very concerned and I tried to offer some type of help. "Would you like a glass of water or a can of soda?" "Would you like a candy bar? " He said, "No, thanks, I'm fine." As we talked I could see that the man's friend was far more upset than he was.

"I was just standing in the dungeon listening to Katie tell about the ghosts when a force pushed past me, seemed to hit me in the forehead and I suddenly sat down—hard. I looked up and saw everyone staring at me with fear in their eyes and told them I was OK." He explained that as the force came past him, it caused his legs to give out. He emphasized that the force didn't push him backwards it just forced him to sit down. "The only thing that hurts now is my butt from sitting down so hard," he explained.

October 30, 2004
"We were just walking around in the dungeon," said a man who was with a friend on the Ghost Tour, "when we saw a board move across a cell. We both saw it at the same time and there was nothing there to move the board."

October 30, 2004
During the Ghost Tour, one guide asked for help with a group who were talking and laughing so loudly that others on the tour could not hear, so I went to ask the group to be a bit quieter.

One women told me her teenage daughter didn't feel well and didn't like the darkness in the cell block. I invited the daughter back to the gift shop where it was brighter, and she nervously followed me. After a few minutes, the girl told Tom that she had seen someone standing upstairs in the back of the cell block and she didn't want to go back. He assured her that what she saw was only the mannequin we had placed on the gallows for effect. She reluctantly went back to the cell block with Tom and he turned on the overhead lights so she could see the mannequin more clearly.

"No," the 18-year-old stated emphatically as she pointed to the second floor of the cell block. "That's not what I saw—I saw a woman dressed in purple with white hair standing up there," she stated while pointing to the second level of the cell block above the gallows. Turning on her heel, the teenager practically ran out of the cell block. By the time her mother and the others joined her, she was a bit calmer, but she was definitely ready to leave.

October 30, 2004
Even though we did not tell them where other visitors had experienced strange and unusual feelings, several members of the Philadelphia Ghost Hunters Alliance shared their experiences in the jail's dungeon:

A woman saw a man dressed in a "striped suit leaning against the wall" in the first cell to the left of the entrance to the dungeon and also felt a force push her and throw her towards the furnace area. Later that evening she went up to the second floor of the cell block and felt a "force" or "heaviness" near Cell 6.

Another woman said she felt she could sense the names "Charlie" and "John" while she was in the dungeon. *(Charles Sharp and John Donohue were both accused Molly Maguires who were hanged in the jail.)*

October 31, 2004
"As I stood near the furnace, a door opened showing a white light and a shadow of a person came walking out," said Amanda from Lehighton. "Then the door shut and the shadow was gone." Amanda explained that she was not referring to a real door in the dungeon, but a door that appeared to be in the air. She also said her father had told her that her great-grandfather had been beaten in the dungeon and that he had died after he was released.

May 2005
Tom went down to the dungeon to do some work, "As I entered

Gathering of Orbs: *Many size orbs can be seen in the back of the dungeon. The stairway leading to the main cell block is in the right corner.*

I saw someone, or a shadow of someone, go into a dungeon cell. Thinking there was someone there I waited quietly until the person came out so I wouldn't scare the wits out him. I waited, and waited, but no one came out—there was no one there but me."

May 21, 2005

Two young boys, each about 10 years old, went into the cell at the end of the dungeon. They both could see their breath because it was so cold and their flashlight suddenly went out. As they came out of the cell to report this to their guide, Tara, their flashlight turned back on.

May 28, 2005

Steve felt strong energy around him and a shadow on his shoulders during his entire tour. He also felt a strong presence in the dungeon in Cell D6.

June 21, 2005

Five of our teenage guides decided to have a girls' night sleepover at the jail, eat, watch scary movies, have fun and, most importantly, look for ghosts. Ann, an adult guide, agreed to stay with them. Guide Kate later related what had happened in the dungeon, "I was the first one down there and I saw a brown pant leg where no one is supposed to be. It moved off to the left as if somebody was walking and then disappeared. I kept saying to the others, 'Mr. McBride is down here and trying to scare us.' But I found out when I went up to the kitchen that he was up there enjoying our desserts and no one with a brown pant leg was down in the dungeon with us."

June 25, 2005
A group of ten people asked to go back down to the dungeon. "When the guide took us down we were very resistent to go into the dungeon. As we went in, three of us noticed a black, dark shadow swoop from the ceiling and disappear into the floor followed by a loud banging noise. Everyone screamed and ran out frantically. We couldn't breath".

One member, a red-haired woman in her mid-20s, couldn't catch her breath, felt ill, looked as if she were in shock and quickly left the building. She later came back in to ask a question, but soon ran out again, still short of breath.

June 25, 2005
When Alisa, one of our guides, was closing the dungeon for the night, she noticed something strange. "I walked down into the dungeon and a black shadow of a man was in the door of one of the cells. When I looked at it, it went back inside the cell. As I walked from the door to the back of the dungeon it followed me, going in and out of each cell. I was trying not to look because I knew I shouldn't be seeing anything."

Not surprisingly, most of our guides will not close up the dungeon by themselves. When guides first start working for us they are eager to do as asked and dutifully shut off the lights and lock up the dungeon. But very soon, we hear these new guides asking

The "Luxury Cell": Because this is the only dungeon cell with a toilet, the jail's guides have dubbed it the "luxury cell." Note the orbs above and below the lamp and table, which were added for visitor's viewing.

for someone to accompany them on this quick task. In fact, most of our guides would rather dust the display cases than close up the dungeon alone.

July 3, 2005

Our guide Tara noted, "I was taking my tour down to the dungeon when suddenly my throat began to hurt. I tried to talk to my tour but my voice was all screechy and I had to force myself to talk so they could hear me. When we got back up to the cell block, I could hardly talk at all. After the tour when I was complaining to Mr. McBride I realized that my voice was OK."

July 15, 2005

A forty-year-old woman from North Carolina came with a friend. When she walked into the dungeon she saw something move in Cell D6. Additionally, she said she could not breath in the warden's bedrooms on the second floor, even though she is not asthmatic.

Her guide Tara later told us of her conversation with this guest: "When I admitted to her that I was afraid in some parts of the building, she told me not to be afraid, that 'Alex follows us and keeps an eye on us.'" (This conversation between Tara and the

Close-Ups of Orbs: All of the pictures with orbs have been provided by the jail's visitors. See the photo credits on page 121.

woman happened before the part of the tour when Alexander Campbell is mentioned as one of the Molly Maguires who was hanged in the jail.) This woman explained that Alex is happy we tell his story and he protects us from the ghosts who have cruel intentions and want to harm us."

This explanation about the spirits wanting to protect us brought to mind our unusual experience a few years earlier when Tom was oddly kept out of the room were the heated argument was taking place.

July 16, 2005
Liza from Tacoma, WA, felt spirits in several different locations: in the dungeon she saw a long coat with a pant leg and she felt the sensation of rain falling on her back, but she didn't get wet; in the cell block, she saw a wisp, such as that of steam or a cloud, in the area to the right of the gallows; and in the library she heard a thump and saw a book move towards the end of the shelf.

July 17, 2005
Lauren, an attractive blond woman from Levittown, PA, related, "During the tour in the dungeon, I had a strong feeling that some-one or something was telling me to get out. I didn't know what to

make of it. After the tour when I went upstairs, I felt very short of breath and needed to leave that area."

July 31, 2005

A woman, about 55, came to Tom and asked about "odd feelings and things like that." She explained that as she had walked toward the back of the cell block past the stairs, she had gotten terrible goosebumps. As she told us about this feeling, she showed us her arms and said she had goosebumps just thinking about it.

Back in the gift shop, we were chatting and she mentioned that during her tour she had thought of her 20-year-old son at home, and had suddenly became very concerned about him, even though she had seen him just a few hours before. In discussing 20-year-old sons with the woman, Tom remembered that around 1988 a 20-year-old prisoner had committed suicide in his cell. After hearing which cell, she realized that she had thought of her son at the exact time she had passed the cell where this sad event had occurred many years ago. She said she had never before had foreboding feelings about her son and then she hurried out the door.

August 2005

"We had had lots of rain for days, and water had seeped into the dungeon and was on the floor," said guide Kate. "I went down to sweep and clean up the water and as I was sweeping I felt a presence watching me and suddenly something moved past me. I knew I was the only one in the dungeon but I looked around anyway. There was no one else there but me." She continued, "Later on I was in the middle of the dungeon talking with visitors on the tour. I told them about the feelings I had when I was sweeping the water when something kicked me in the ankle! Like someone was telling me to get out of there. Since there was no one standing near me I looked down at my ankle and I noticed the water at my feet was moving. It was swirling and rippling just as if someone had been standing there. There was no wind nor any air movement of any kind in the dungeon, but the water was moving."

August 7, 2005
Standing by the cell in front of the furnace, guide Tara waited in the dungeon for her tour to come down the stairs. All of a sudden she heard the shuffle of feet on the dirty floor and thought someone was standing next to her. "It sounded like someone was dragging his feet and it made a loud noise right beside me," she said. But when she turned to see who was there, she found she was alone and her group had not yet come down the stairs.

August 9, 2005
"I felt a very cool breeze and the hair on my arms raised when we went down in the dungeon. I felt that we were not alone and that the room was crowded with people," said a 45-year-old woman.

August 11, 2005
A man from New York came to the jail and brought several friends with him. As he was purchasing his admission tickets he told us he had been in the jail before and wanted to come back because of his unusual experience. He said he had been videotaping the building and listening to the story of the jail and the Molly Maguires when all of a sudden he felt a stab of electricity go through his stomach area and out his back. He said the force travelled right though him with great energy. He had no idea what had happened but returned that day to see the jail again.

August 17, 2005
"I felt like I was being strangled—actually strangled," a woman told her guide Chelsey. The woman, in her mid-30s, said that as she walked into the dungeon she had this horrible strangling feeling and had to run out to the exercise yard and lay down. She was very distraught, said she could not finish the tour and quickly left.

September 5, 2005
"I tried to take pictures of my husband and two children down in the dungeon. When we looked at the pictures, my family was missing. Only a red and yellow glow was on the picture." This

was related by D. J. of
Rosenhayn, NJ.

September 5, 2005
Although most guides do not
want to be in the dungeon alone,
one day Lauren ventured down
by herself. "The first time I was
down there it felt like something
was standing by me. Today on
my first tour I saw two small
green lights towards the bottom
of a cell. On the second tour
today a large green slash of light
flashed across the top of the
cell." Lauren said she's not sure
if she wants to be in the dungeon alone anymore.

*Along for the Tour: An orb joins
visitors on their tour.*

Fall 2005
Members of the Tamaqua Paranormal Research Society took their
video and recording equipment to the center of the dungeon as
part of their search for spirits in the Old Jail. Paul and Kieran had
their video cameras all charged up and another member had a
voice recorder. Because they had searched in other locations, they
had prepared for this visit and had new and fully charged batteries. But as they moved to the middle of the main hallway, all three
pieces of equipment shut off at the same time. They thought,
"Oh, well, we might as well move on," and walked to the back of
the dungeon. Suddenly, the recorder and cameras all turned back
on at the same time.

Meanwhile, two other members, Jeff and Larry, had walked to a
hallway with their video camera filming as they walked. Suddenly,
a long board that was standing in a corner flew several feet across
the hallway and landed against the opposite wall. As Jeff backed

up in surprise something brushed the back of his head. He thought it must be a string or a piece of hanging material, but when he turned around to brush it aside, he discovered there was nothing behind his head. He said later how excited he was that his camera had caught the mysterious movement of the board.

A short while later another member, Cheryl, complained of not feeling well. She became extremely upset for no apparent reason and decided to leave the dungeon.

October 8, 2005
Aaron, a 35-year-old from Hagerstown, MD, said he was not a big believer in ghosts but that he did believe in spirits. As soon as he entered the dungeon he was drawn towards a cell, and as he entered the cell he felt a presence pull him further in. The tour was moving on, so he left the cell to rejoin the tour. A few minutes after he left the building he came back and told me he did not feel right leaving because "something" was not over. He asked if he could go back into the dungeon, so we had one of our guides take him down.

Aaron went back into the same cell and stood for a few minutes. He told us he felt a man was there, laying in the back corner. He said this man seemed lonely and just wanted some comfort. Then he felt cold air come around him, although he did not feel threatened. His left hand became very hot with pin pricks all over it. He told us he felt the presence in the cell is unable to rest because something "really bad had happened in there."

October 8, 2005
Joe told us he had lived in several houses that were "haunted" and wanted to tell us what he had experienced on the tour. When he entered the dungeon he felt the presence of a woman who had experienced a difficult time there. Then as he went into Cell D6 he became extremely cold, even though, he explained, he is nor-

mally a very warm person. He could also sense a strong female presence in this cell.

October 18, 2005

As the tour went into the dungeon, a man about 45 years old looked towards the back of the jail. Just as he was glancing away, he saw a green fluorescent light to the right of the furnace by the wall. He couldn't figure out what it was, so he shut his eyes tightly and then opened them again, only to find the green light shape was still there about waist high. Later, as this man was telling us about the strange light, a woman in his group said, "Why didn't you say something then? I saw the green light, too, but didn't want to mention it to anyone." Then two others in their group said they, too, had seen the green light in the dungeon but felt weird commenting on it. We assured them we had not put a green light in the dungeon.

October 22, 2005

After completing their tour a group of teenage girls, accompanied by a father, asked to go back into the dungeon. Tom took them down, and the girls entered one of the cells. Samantha, one of the teenagers, said her heart began to race, and the others said they felt uneasy and that they should get out of the cell.

Leaving that cell, they decided to go into the next one. But when they entered they heard moaning and a clear voice said "Move! Get out!" And something pushed them toward the door. Samantha's father went into the cell and, although he did not hear anything, he said he had a feeling of trepidation and that they should not be in that cell. They all left in a big hurry!

October 29, 2005

Here we go again with the cell door that refuses to stay closed! One guest on the Ghost Tour had just heard the guide explain about the door of one cell that won't stay closed. "I'm going to close the cell door anyway," the man said to his wife. As he was closing the door he looked away to talk to another person when something caught his eye. He realized that the cell door had started to reopen! He was quite startled and didn't touch the door again.

October 29, 2005
We received this note from a young woman following her Ghost Tour:

October 2005
"I was in the cell and stood stiff and I started to get really warm. Then suddenly something or someone was tugging at my hair. I told one of my friends not to scare me, but I found he wasn't there."

October 29, 2005
"I was looking into a cell in the dungeon while everyone was ahead of me. All of a sudden I felt someone touch me. I asked my friend if any of them had touched me and they each said, 'No!'" reported a guest on evening's Ghost Tour.

October 29, 2005
A family who had been with a ghost hunting group from Philadelphia came for a regular tour the day after their ghost hunting session. At breakfast that morning they had been listening to the recording they had made in the dungeon the previous night and could clearly hear the voice of a very young girl saying, "Help me, help me!" I told the group that others in the past had reported a woman calling those same words, but they all insisted that this was not a woman's voice, it was that of a young girl.

Chapter 6

Thoughts & Reflections

by Joe P.

Joe P. first visited the Old Jail shortly after it opened as a museum in 1995. The Hazleton, PA, man came for a tour and then spent a long period of time quietly sitting in the cell block. After a while he asked for a piece of paper to record his feelings and thoughts about the building and the men who died here, so I gave him an ordinary piece of note paper. His thoughts were many and deep, and he soon returned to borrow a legal size pad.

Joe continues to visit the jail several times a year and each visit brings new insights with his interpretation of the emotions and activity flowing from this mysterious building. The following pages contain a sampling of Joe's thoughts and reflections.

July 11, 1997

Thank you for letting me record my impression of the Mauch Chunk jail. As soon as you walk the winding street leading up to the jail "IT" (the feeling) begins. About a block and a half from its entrance you can begin to see its darkened walls. You begin to feel labored breathing and a very heavy step. It is literally pulling you in. By the time you are inside the lobby of the jail you feel you are in another time. The feeling of being in a far away past stays with you the entire time you walk the premises.

Starting with the steps leading down to the basement dungeon you immediately begin to feel light-headed and almost a sense of weightlessness. As soon as you enter the dungeon itself you are hit with the cold blasts of air and a dark, sinister and overwhelming sadness and psychic pain. The first four dungeon cells on the opposite side of the entrance strike me as where the most violent and insane met their fate. Each dungeon cell is like a Rorschach test. Each cell is totally different with its own characteristics and personality. If I could sum up the dungeon, it is cold, dark, dangerous and alive with grief and evil. A coiled snake awaiting the wrong, misguided soul who walks without reverence for this place.

As you walk up from the dungeon the feeling of oppression is less pronounced in its hostile sadness, a different level of vibration. On the first floor is a feeling of unfocused energy with less a feeling of hopelessness and more a sense of active energy.

Cell 17 speaks for itself. While I would not want to stay in the cell overnight, I get a feeling of tranquility when I gaze at the hand-print. Here is a true miracle. In the midst of hell on earth, with the worst offerings of humankind breathing this air Cell 17 stands as a testament to the laws of justice. It is an uneasy shrine, but a shrine nevertheless to anyone with the sensitivity to look past the surface and look deeply and closely into the story the handprint tells. Its mirage, its echo, haunts anyone who is willing to look past the cold logic and rational heart of the skeptic.

If the atmosphere on the first floor is less focused, the second floor is VERY focused in certain spots. The library feels hot, then cold, then hot. It feels oppressive and aggressive within the room. The light almost looks and feels "cloudy". It is hard to breath and walk. Whenever I walked in to this room my hands, neck and shoulders would tingle. I feel there is an active intelligence operating in this room. I do not feel alone in this room.

- continued -

- continued -

*As you walk out of the library you are imme-
diately struck by how different the atmosphere is compared to the dungeon and the
first floor. When you round the corner as
soon as you get by the window, you get light-
headed and dizzy. Cell #6 and the last cell
after it seem unusually bad or haunted.
These two cells seem the most "restless"
outside of the library and dungeon. As you
walk past Cell #6 there is a scent of flowers
or perfume. As I walk the top floor I can
hear the echo of profanity, screams, wails
and howls of derision at the guards on duty.
I sense the weight and torment the guard
felt every moment he walked the premises.*

*This jail is sacred ground . . . a psychic pow-
erhouse. This jail will stand forever as a
testament to the spirit of a man that not
even nature could destroy.*

     Sincerely,
     Joe P.

September 15, 1997

The less congested with people the jail is the more energy the spirits, ghosts, etc., will have to generate. But there are and will be certain cases where you could have a spectacular occurrence with a hundred people in the building.

As I entered the library today I felt cold and had the feeling of being watched.

The second floor of the cell block brought on a feeling of nausea when turning the corner up to Cell #6, that is, around the area where the hangings occurred.

Cell 17 deals with people on an intense, individual level to the interested. For most it might not be any big deal, to some it could be an inspiration, and to a few a bad sense of foreboding if they don't change their ways. These reactions might take days, weeks, months, even years to sink in. The hand on the wall is "happy" that this jail is now open to all who want to grasp its subtle, eternal message.

The hand on the wall seems to be saying, at least whispering in my ear today as I sit staring at cell 17 and writing this letter, "Thank You" to Mr. and Mrs. McBride who have honored the past and for that eternity smiles.

Thanks for your time,
Joe P.

June 27, 1998

During the Mass it seemed for each living person there were ten dead spirits, all relatives and friends of you who came to honor the past, who hovered over everyone's head and shoulders. The air was thick with dead people no longer in pain but free to lovingly accept your prayers. I could see energy rising out of everyone in attendance like the hot, hazy bright sun bounding off the roofs of cars permitting you to see the invisible waves rising up into the air. As the energy flow of the living rose up the spirits drank it up and wallowed in it like when you jump into the warm, heated ocean of August right after dusk. These are not the trapped souls that infest your jail. These are the souls who can interact when they see fit. They are free and they had the best spiritual banquet in their honor possible.

At one point during the Mass as I redirected my eyes from the booklet, while taking in the mental image of the gallows, the priest and the attendants, a clear bolt of pure white energy shot through the uppermost window behind the gallows into the left upper level directly towards the first three cells. I assumed someone had snapped an intense flash bulb, or the video man was trying to induce a show of light for dramatic effect

In Remembrance: The anniversary of the hanging of the Molly Maguires is commemorated every year with a Mass and Remembrance Ceremony in the Old Jail.

and, therefore, I assumed this was a refracted image from a closed window. The window, I realized later, was open.

Please let me know when I return sometime later this summer if the video man caught any flashing light. I'm not claiming anything except for the fact that something startled my senses in a direct, three dimensional way that my memory refuses to suppress.

Joe P.

November 1, 1998

I wanted to tell you that several spots in the jail are getting "soaked" with the smell of lilac. In fact, the second before I started writing this down the soft smell surrounded me once again.

For the first time I can remember the warden's room [living room] had a pronounced lilac perfume smell. It also had a strong male presence who "lorded" over the room. Whoever this male spirit is, he gives off very arrogant airs.

About one-half hour after the first encounter I went back to the warden's room and the lilac smell hit me even stronger. The second area of lilacs is the front door of the Jail cells. I've gotten this identical energy for about five or six times at this spot.

Thanks again,
Joe P.

Authors' note: While writing this letter, Joe was sitting at a picnic table by the first cell on the left—at one time a barbershop.

June 13, 1999

The cell [women's block] on the 2nd floor contains two mannequins. The one is able to stare at the mirror on the wall. It is a very unnerving feeling to watch the eyes of this mannequin almost follow you around. All of the bad energy from the cells in this block is contained in the eyes of this mannequin. The air is thick and heavy around this doll (of the dead). For most people this area is no problem, but for some kids and some adults it should generate a creepy feeling of being watched by a malevolent spirit.

As I write this I suddenly looked over at Cell #17. It seems different. All of a sudden a light chill and darkness is in the air. I am aware of death. When I exhale I can sense its presence.

I feel no need to go down to the dungeon. The 2nd floor seemed to take over today. It's a strong area for feeling energy.

One more thing, I still smell that lilac on the 2nd floor landing by the women's cell block area. It almost never fails.

Joe P.

July 30, 1999

A circle of energy around the upstairs at the gallows section. Feels like an electric current in a slow river flow—does not feel bad but seems to attract the emotions of the people who were hanged on the gallows.

The gallows are so exactingly created. They resonate with a flow of spirit energy that has rested on this area because of its sanctified ground.

The Jail seems to split itself into separate, distinct "personalities" or areas each of which has a different energy or character.

1) The handprint and the gallows area create a religious aspect in an unlikely place—a jail.

2) The upstairs has lots of "ghosts" by the library and the 2nd floor women's section.

3) And, of course, the dungeon remains the dark soul of the prison. It seems to delight in welcoming new staff to the realities of the Old Mauch Chunk Jail.

It (the jail) can push and pull, bite and scratch, and even whisper or shout. It can make you dizzy, nauseous and ready to faint. You feel you are walking in cement. Time can play tricks on you. Never approach this place with anything less than respect. And never go down into the dungeon alone after the sun goes down.

The dungeon feeds off energy. Never dare or tempt it. Never try to call up its presence. It is a swirling mass of poisoned air beyond any hope of forgiveness. The more people congregate in the dungeon area at the same time the more likely less bad problems. Strength in number maybe?

The Jail is now more interesting, more restored and more powerful as a living interactive museum. Treat it with respect and it speaks to you in many voices and in ways beyond my comprehension. Its historical importance has only just begun.

Thanks,
Joe P.

September 5, 1999

A strong presence of beer emanating from the area next to the Visitors' Room all the way to the door facing the outside courtyard. Someone must have been a chronic alcoholic who would look out the door. As I write this I'm getting a strong smell of rotten eggs for a couple seconds at a time, then it goes away and I sense a smell of flowers. Good and evil?

I think the Visitors' Room not only has a "cigar" ghost but also a "beer" or alcoholic ghost in the area I described. Maybe the BBC will capture something when they come here. The dungeon, the gallows area, especially upstairs, the library, the shower room are "hot spots" of energy.

The handprint on the wall stands by itself. A unique moment in time captured forever. It is never a "bad" spot. The very fact that it exists is all it needs to "be".

Joe P.

Authors' note: Joe was sitting at a picnic table in the cell block while writing. The British Broadcasting Company, BBC, produced a one-hour program on unsolved mysteries; the mysterious handprint was one 12-minute segment of this program. Unfortunately, we never had the opportunity to see their footage or the finished program.

June 4, 2000

The first floor looks like it was "cleansed" over the winter and is now unfolding like a budding plant or flower. The place is LIVE and filled with energy (what else is new!) But it is a different energy from last year. It is more inviting on the surface. The ghosts or spirits are wanting to flex their muscles and are just starting to unwind. They enjoy the respect and awareness this town provides.

The constant telling of their story (Molly Maguires) is an offering, a gift. But if the first floor seems more "bright" because of the gallows acting as a shrine to their brave efforts, the second floor seems "heavy" with spirits. Very thick and pronounced like a ghost fog.

And now we come to the dungeon. It never ceases to amaze me how active and aggressive its "vibe" is. It's cold, too cold for June down there. Those round holes in the wall resemble the empty eye sockets of a brooding skull. It's almost like the dungeon will attempt to over compensate for any brightness on the upper floors. Being alone in the dungeon invites the spirit to interact. Even more, the level of fear caused by being alone intensifies the effect.

It seems that more people are bringing cameras, which could mean a constant source of new

- continued -

- continued -

business. Why? As more people snap pictures, more opportunities present themselves for interesting interaction between the Jail's energy and the energy of the people taking the shots. Every new photograph with wavy lines, smoky clouds, filters, etc. are unique testimonials to the aura of the Old Jail.

After many documentaries and features don't you honestly feel that there has never been an accurate, respectful and cohesive portrayal to suit your tastes? Each one had an agenda that would cloud the issues and leave an unsatisfied feeling about each venture. Maybe as time goes by the media will become more accurate and coherent in its spin of the story.

I'm sure you realize this place operates on a least three, sometimes conflicting, levels. History, Religion and yes, though more people don't want to deal with it, the Supernatural level. Because of this it is sometimes difficult to juggle these three forces because the energies are very conflicting.

History is very tainted by The Old Jail. Religion also has a bumpy road in the story. Not all the Church power was directed at the *"good fight" at times, so the tale becomes a raw nerve of class distinction and prejudice. If this potent brew wasn't enough, the realm of the twilight zone, the one step beyond world, beckons for some. For many people, the Jail is an interactive museum with an extra reality that introduces itself in too many ways for me to even imagine. A history buff may not be interested in the religious aspect while both might be threatened by the supernatural aspect. This mix of tourists produces an interesting mix, but my guess is over a period of time it will be the 3rd type of patron that will give the jail its everlasting fame.*

Over a period of time a consensus tends to develop. Even in this short time the jail has been opened the number of occurrences, incidents, strange photography, ghosts, voices, noises, smells, etc. have given the Jail legitimate claim as an important psychic hot spot. How you can achieve the delicate balance will be your constant duty and privilege.

Your friend,
Joe P.

July 11, 2000

I visited with my sister, her 12 year-old daughter and her daughter's friend. When we were in the dungeon all of us and two other people on the tour heard a two syllable beat from within Cell #2 on the far side away from the steps. I was closest to the sound and questioned the rest of the people immediately if they also heard that noise. Everyone agreed it came from the cell and that it was no trick. Everyone had their own reaction, but it's fair to say the tour was buzzing after that.

My niece and her friend immediately approached the tour guide (new kid) to get his reaction. He told them he felt "numb" when he looked in the direction of the noise. It is interesting he used that term. Seventeen years ago I went to visit a friend in Virginia. He lived in a haunted house that actually attacked me with an unseen force that left me paralyzed or "numb." My then fiance had to punch me and got us out of the house. We sat outside in her car for an hour until my friend and his wife got back home.

If anyone smells lilacs or flowers I think it's the young girl other little girls have spoken about to their parents.

From recent research I've dug up the fact that in the supernatural world the smell of flowers is a "good" spirit, one who is reaching out in a positive way. That's not to say caution should not always prevail, but ghosts and spirits and energies come in all shapes and sizes.

Till next time - Joe

~ Chapter 7 ~

Conclusion

T en years ago, when we bought this grand building, we had no idea what awaited us inside these walls. Our main focus was to preserve history—both the history of the Molly Maguires and the history of this stone prison. For many years we concentrated on the Molly Maguire story and wanted the jail to be known for its connection to these important figures in American history. Apparently, though, the jail has many, many more stories it wants to share. We realize now that the jail has been teaching us its own version of history. Before we bought the jail, we never considered the possibility that the building might have ghosts or spirits, and today, we are still baffled by the bizarre events narrated to us by our visitors.

Our three daughters are disappointed that not one of them has ever experienced anything peculiar in the Old Jail. Frankly, Tom and I are relieved we haven't. For all the hours we spend alone in this building, it's probably best that our experiences are limited to the realm of the visible and known. Through the years Tom and I each have had our favorite stories but we had subsequently forgotten many of the details in the reports. Compiling the stories into a book form has reminded us of these moments and has helped put the descriptions into perspective.

The interesting and unexplained activity in the jail has ebbed and flowed over the years. There was an initial flourish of extrasensory activity when we first opened our doors to visitors. Then we would often go for weeks without hearing about anything unusual happening in the building. This would be followed by a period of renewed activity and reports.

The jail seems to have an effect on a wide range of senses, both emotional and physical. Visitors have reported an array of sensations: emotional feelings such as uneasiness, apprehension and foreboding; physical ramifications such as a heart beating faster, profuse sweating, hands shaking and extreme shortness of breath; and sensory effects such as the smell of smoke or flowers, the sight of a moving object or the figure of a person, the sound of wailing or yelling and the feeling of an icy breeze or a kick to the back of the knee.

Since our early days we have been aware that certain areas of the jail—the library, the dungeon, Cell 6 and Cell 17, in particular—seem to generate a great deal of activity. But it still amazes us just how many similarities these first-hand accounts have to each other. Many visitors get pushed in the library, hear cursing in the dungeon, have trouble walking in Cell 6, and see or hear men in Cell 17.

In compiling and rereading these tales, a few details have emerged that we had not previously noticed. The color purple seems to have a meaning: women wearing purple have reported odd happenings; and some visitors have seen a woman wearing purple. Certain smells have been noted repeatedly, namely the smell of flowers and the smell of rotten eggs. Men with the name "Tom" seem particularly open to experiencing the jail's strange phenomena. And, perhaps most interestingly, children's experiences are prone to be drastically differently than those of adults.

Whereas adults often times feel foreboding and distressful emotions, children seem to feel only intrigue and, oddly, comfort. Girls, around 10 to 12, and boys, around 10, seem to be the most affected, and they tend to be genuinely curious rather than fearful. We've noticed that every spring several young girls tell us that as they walked through the jail, particularly in the area of the hangings or the dungeon, each could feel the heaviness of an invisible hand on her shoulder. The girls are never frightened and explain the hand as a "guiding hand" or like "that of a friend."

Month after month, year after year, unsuspecting visitors to the Old Jail report that their tours provided them with an experience like no other. Readers may now want to hustle off to Jim Thorpe to hunt for ghosts in the Old Jail, but they should remember the majority of people who have searched for spirits here have never found them. Ghosts apparently don't work on schedules or at someone's bidding. Ghost hunters and students of parapsychology have rarely encountered the spirits in the Old Jail; the spirits have manifested themselves to the majority of people without encouragement.

Since the Old Jail's story is apparently not finished, we will not attempt to offer a conclusion. We will let the jail tell its own story in its own way. Our decade-long adventure with the jail, though, has provided many more questions than it has answers. We never thought we'd be pondering such unanswerable questions: *Are there spirits or ghosts in the Old Jail? Are they the ghosts of the Molly Maguires? Why are they still here? Do they have unfinished business? Are we supposed to learn something from them? Is the handprint on the wall of Cell 17 a testament to the fact that an innocent man was put to death? Or are our own minds playing tricks on us?*

Although we don't know the answers to such questions and we probably never will, we will continue to record for posterity the strange and unreal happenings in the Old Jail for as long as the Jail wants to make its stories known.

The Old Jail Museum

128 West Broadway
Jim Thorpe, PA 18229
570-325-5259

Tours Daily *(closed Wednesdays)*
Memorial Day Weekend
through Labor Day

12:00 noon to 4:30 p.m.
(final tour at 4:30 p.m.)

Weekends only:
September and October

Closed:
November to Memorial Day

~ About the Authors ~

Betty Lou McBride was born in Cleveland, Ohio. Her mother's family originated in Limerick, Ireland. A graduate of Notre Dame Academy in Cleveland, Betty Lou worked for many years as a legal secretary in a private law practice. In 1968 she married Thomas E. McBride of Junedale, Pennsylvania, whose family came from County Donegal, Ireland. For 13 years Tom and Betty Lou resided in Naples, Florida, where Tom was a Realtor® with his own real estate office.

Betty Lou McBride

In 1981 the family moved to Jim Thorpe, PA. One year later, venturing into something new, they opened The Treasure Shop, a general gift and Irish import shop, in the Mauch Chunk Historic District of Jim Thorpe.

Because numerous members of Betty Lou's family had been employed by railroads (her great-grandfather and granduncle were both victims of rail disasters) and the McBride family had labored in the area's anthracite coal mines, they were naturally drawn to the tragic epic of the Molly Maguires. In 1995 they purchased the former Carbon County Prison where seven of the Irish Molly Maguires had been hanged and opened it for tours as The Old Jail Museum and Heritage Center, Inc.

The Treasure Shop was purchased in 1997 by their daughter, Peggy Dart. Together with her husband, Vince, and son, Blaine, she lives in Jim Thorpe where she continues to operate The Treasure Shop. Daughter, Michelle, also lives in the area and is the owner and operator of Burgundy Hollow, a horse training farm specializing in carriage driving.

Although not a professional writer Betty Lou has written many newspaper articles and informational material over the years. Her previously published booklet, *The Old Jail and the Molly Maguires*, has been in publication since 1996.

Kathleen M. Sisack

Kathleen McBride Sisack graduated from Marian Catholic High School in Tamaqua, PA, and she earned a Bachelor of Arts degree in communications with minors in writing and business from King's College in Wilkes-Barre, PA.

She has had numerous articles and photographs published, including a feature-length cover story in *Ireland of the Welcomes*, published by the Irish Tourist Board, and a chapter in *The Hard Coal Docket* by Judge John P. Lavelle.

Kathleen operates her own graphics and website design business in southeastern Wisconsin. She is currently pursuing a Master of Arts degree in counseling at Lakeland College, where her husband, Christian, teaches English. They reside in Sheboygan, WI, with their cat, Puck, and their Labrador retriever, Oberon.

~ Photo Credits ~

The following books on the Molly Maguires are available at

𝒯𝒽𝑒 𝒯𝓇𝑒𝒶𝓈𝓊𝓇𝑒 𝒮𝒽𝑜𝓅

44 Broadway, Jim Thorpe, PA
1-800-833-1782 • www.IrishTreasureShop.com

Old Jail Museum & the Molly Maguires
by Betty Lou McBride
12 page booklet

Brief history of the Molly Maguires, including description of the seven men hanged in *The Old Jail Museum,* and the history of *The Old Jail Museum* building.

A Molly Maguire Story
by Patrick Campbell
Soft cover, 192 pages

Campbell's search of the history, trial and hanging as a Molly Maguire of his grand-uncle, Alexander Campbell.

Making Sense of the Molly Maguires
by Kevin Kenny
Soft cover, 336 pages

Combining social and cultural history, a portrait of the Molly Maguires; gives us flesh and blood men, their passions and grievances, the crimes they committee and the crimes committed against them.

A Guide to the Molly Maguires
by H.T. Crown & Mark T. Major
Soft cover, 234 pages

Designed to map out important places, people and events of the Molly Maguire era.

A Molly Maguire on Trial,
The Thomas Munley Story by H.T. Crown
Soft cover, 181 pages

Narrative of the background and trial of Thomas Munley, an accused Molly Maguire

The Hard Coal Docket
by John P. Lavelle
Hardbound, 428 pages

Includes 155 pages on the Molly Maguires including the jury selection process and trials.

Who Killed Franklin Gowen?
by Patrick Campbell
Soft cover, 193 pages

An indepth analysis of the 1889 death of Franklin B. Gowen, President of the Reading Railroad and leader in the prosecution of the Molly Maguires.

The Molly Maguires
by Anthony Bimba
Soft cover, 137 pages

In 1932, Bimba reconstructed a "forgotten chapter" in the history of American labor.